presentationzen
DESIGN

A simple visual approach to presenting in today's world

Garr Reynolds

VOICES THAT MATTER™

Presentation Zen Design, Second Edition
A Simple Visual Approach to Presenting in Today's World
Garr Reynolds

New Riders
www.newriders.com

To report errors, please send a note to errata@peachpit.com
New Riders is an imprint of Peachpit, a division of Pearson Education
Copyright © 2014 by Garr Reynolds

Senior Editor: Karyn Johnson
Production Editor: Katerina Malone
Copy Editor: Kelly Kordes Anton
Compositors: Garr Reynolds, Danielle Foster
Proofreader: Rebecca Rider
Indexer: Jack Lewis
Design Consultants: Mayumi Nakamoto, Mimi Heft
Book and Cover Design: Garr Reynolds

ISBN-13: 978-0-321-93415-4
ISBN-10:   0-321-93415-6

9 8 7 6 5 4 3 2 1

Printed and bound in the United States of America

To our children, who remind us always
to embrace the beginner's mind.

Table of Contents

Photo: TEDxKyoto, Mai Morokawa.

Acknowledgments

This book would not have been possible without a lot of help and support. I'd like to thank the following people for their contributions and encouragement:

Nancy Duarte and Mark Duarte and all the wonderful staff at Duarte, Inc., in Silicon Valley, including Paula Tesch and Tracy Barba, for their support.

At New Riders: My great editor Karyn Johnson for her fantastic suggestions and unbelievable patience. Mimi Heft for her help with the design and the cover. Katerina Malone (production editor) for her talent and patience, as well as Danielle Foster for her great production work. Sara Jane Todd for her wonderful marketing efforts.

Guy Kawasaki, Seth Godin, Daniel Pink, Jim Quirk, and Deryn Verity for their enlightened advice and content in the early stages of the process.

To Jumpei Matsuoka and all the cool people at both iStockphoto.com and Pixta for their tremendous support with the images and the special offers that are included at the back of this book.

Designer Mayumi Nakamoto for always being there when I need her.

The Design Matters Japan and business community, including Toru Yamada, Shigeki Yamamoto, Tom Perry, Darren Saunders, Daniel Rodriguez, David Baldwin, Nathan Bryan, Jiri Mestecky, Doug Schafer, Barry Louie, Michael Bobrove, and Keizo Yamada. Thanks to Markuz Wernli Saito for his beautiful garden photos. To Daniel Kwintner and IDA Japan for their contribution.

To Patrick Newell for his contribution and friendship.

A special thanks to Scott Kelby, John McWade, Maureen Stone, Stephen Few, David S. Rose, and Nancy Duarte for their very kind contributions to the book.

Back in the States, a big thank you to those who contributed ideas and support, including Debbie Thorn, CZ Robertson, and to my buddies in Silicon Valley, Ric Bretschneider and Howard Cooperstein. Also to Mark and Liz Reynolds for picking me up in the snow.

Thank you to Mark Templeton and the amazing folks at Citrix.

I'd like to thank the thousands of subscribers to the Presentation Zen blog and to all the blog readers who have contacted me over the years to share their stories and examples, including Les Posen in Australia and Olivia Mitchell in New Zealand.

A very big thank you to Reiko Hiromoto at Kansai Gaidai University for her insights and suggestions.

Although I could not include all the slides in this book, I want to thank all the people who submitted sample slides, including Jeff Brenman, Pierre Morsa, Scott B. Schwertly, Dr. Aisyah Saad Abdul Rahim, Marty Neumeier, Nancy Duarte, Naveen Sinha, Dr. Bonnie Bassler, and Elissa Fink and all the talented guys at Tableau Software.

And of course my biggest supporter in all of this is my wife Ai, who is always understanding and supportive (and who kept me well fed, too).

I am blessed indeed to be surrounded by such great people. Hontoni Arigatou!

introduction

The ability to simplify means to eliminate the unnecessary so that the necessary may speak.

— Hans Hofmann

Design Matters

Presentation and design lessons are all around us, even in something as seemingly unrelated as a beautifully prepared traditional Japanese meal. A few years ago on a late fall afternoon, a friend and I were walking along *Tetsugaku no Michi* (Philosopher's Road) in the city of Kyoto. After our walk, we stopped in a local restaurant for a traditional meal. Japanese-style meals are called *washoku*. The kanji characters for washoku (和食) literally represent "harmony" and "food," and harmony is indeed a key principle embodied in Japanese traditional cooking.

In Japan, food is about experience as much as it is about sustenance. Although this particular restaurant was nothing special or extraordinary for Japan, I was (as always) impressed by the presentation of the meal. How can the presentation be so profound, I thought, without hardly a trace of decorative or nonessential elements? Clearly, presentation matters.

Washoku is guided by simple principles that lead to harmony and balance in terms of both nutrition and aesthetics. For example, *go shiki* (five colors) dictates that meals have a variety of colors: red, green, yellow, black, and white. This not only ensures good nutrition, but it also leads to a visually appealing display. The principle of *go kan* (five senses) suggests that the cook think about touch, sound, smell, and, of course, sight in addition to taste and nutrition. How the meal looks is, in many ways, as important as how it tastes. "We are as nourished by the presentation as we are nourished by the food," says John Daido Loori in *The Zen of Creativity* (Random House, 2005).

Other guiding principles of washoku include *go mi* (five tastes), leading to a balance of flavors; *go ho* (five ways), which encourages a variety of cooking methods; and *go kan mon* (five outlooks), guidelines concerning respect and appreciation for the meal and the spirit in which it is to be consumed. In Japan, lessons about the art of presentation are everywhere, sometimes in very unexpected places indeed.

Left: Philosopher's Road in Kyoto, Japan.

If we open our eyes and are willing to think differently, we can see lessons all around. Similar to a designer, a washoku preparer is guided by principles that help in the careful decisions of what to include and what to exclude. Ingredients may depend on many things, including the season and occasion. Proportions are measured with restraint and are in balance with one another. Above all, elements are chosen and arranged visually to be in balance and harmony from the point of view of the customer.

Balance, harmony, restraint, simplicity, and naturalness. These are some of the guiding principles behind the preparation of washoku. These are also fundamental principles that we can apply to design and the art of presentation outside the culinary world. Design matters.

Who Is This Book For?

For those of us who are not trained as professional designers, the world of design and graphic design may seem mysterious. We know what we like when we see it, but we lack the visual literacy to articulate our thoughts, let alone attempt to create these designs ourselves. For many of us, there is a hole in our education when it comes to visual communication. This book is designed to help you obtain a better understanding of design that you can use to communicate your ideas in your life and work. Because one of the most common forms of communication is presentation slides, that is the medium discussed in this book.

This book is not for professionally trained designers. This is for all the other professionals—such as educators, businesspeople, leaders of organizations, and even students—who recognize that we live in a time in which knowledge of design and visual communication skills are increasingly valued. The goal of this book is to increase your awareness of visual communication as it relates to multimedia presentations. After you read this book, you should be able to

1. Understand some basic concepts of graphic design, which will allow you to work more effectively with professional designers.
2. Create better visuals.
3. Communicate better in your presentations.

You'll be able to design better presentation visuals, but even more importantly, you will be able to apply principles learned here to other disciplines in which visual communication is significant.

It's a new, visual world

Tools are commonplace, but knowledge is not. In the past, the tools for creating high-quality graphics and multimedia presentations belonged only to a select few. Today, those tools are in the hands of virtually everyone with a computer. However, possessing the hardware and software tools and knowing how to operate them does not a designer make. Many schools and training facilities offer classes on learning the technical tools, which are pretty straightforward. But, with the exception of creative arts programs, few classes cover design concepts and the fundamentals of graphic design.

What we should focus on are not the tools and software techniques, but the principles and elements of visuals communication that lead to better design—whether you use digital tools or not. Without knowledge of basic visual communication principles, it's very easy to let the software templates take you places you really don't want to go. In the world of presentations, too much of what passes for visuals in the boardroom and in the classroom is nothing more than a collection of recycled bullets, corporate templates, clip art, and seemingly random charts and graphs. To make it worse, the charts and graphs are often too detailed or cluttered to make effective onscreen visuals or are too vague to stand alone as quality documentation.

Toward a new kind of literacy

A professional or student in the 21st century needs to have a good degree of multimedia literacy. While the tools of the day are ephemeral, an understanding of the principles and techniques found in the broad field of visual communication is the thing of real and lasting value. George Lucas says that visual communication, or multimedia literacy, should be an integral part of teaching and learning in schools. Lucas states that what we typically call "the arts" should also be taught in the regular communication classes where students learn practical applications of graphics, music, various visual arts, and language to tell a story, to sell an idea, to persuade, to question, and so on.

In a 2012 interview with the educational foundation Edutopia (www.edutopia.org), Martin Scorsese says that people today—young people especially—need to understand the power of design and visual communication: "[Young people] need to know how ideas and emotions are expressed through a visual form," says Scorsese. "We have to begin to teach younger people how to use this very powerful tool...because we know the image can be so strong, not only for good use, but for bad use. Film is very powerful—images are very powerful—and we need to teach younger people how to use them....or at least how to interpret them."

In *The New York Times*–best-selling book *A Whole New Mind* (Riverhead Trade, 2005), Daniel Pink makes it clear that design is a key aptitude for professionals and students to develop and nurture. "Cultivating a design sensibility," says Pink, "can even make the world a little bit better. When people become more aware of the world around them and how design and design thinking impacts that world, they begin to see how designers are really change agents, they design ways to make the world better."

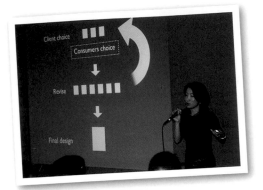

Presentations and design

If your ideas matter—if your business plans, your research results, or your cause are worth spreading—then design and presentation matter. "The more people who know your idea the more powerful it becomes," says business guru Seth Godin. Solid oral presentation amplified through the effective use of multimedia and good design is a powerful way to spread your message. If you can present well, you will be doing your cause—and those who share your cause—a great service. Presentations are not everything, but they are one thing that can make a big difference in getting your message out. When you're trying to change the world, there is no excuse for being boring and there is no excuse for poorly designed visuals.

In *The Designful Company: How to Build a Culture of Nonstop Innovation* (New Riders, 2009), designer Marty Neumeier makes the case for the power of design inside organizations to inspire change. Neumeier explains how we can build a culture of change that embraces design by focusing on 16 key levers such as weaving a story, bringing design management inside the organization, introducing parallel thinking, recognizing talent and creativity, and so on. Neumeier also believes we should "ban PowerPoint." He means, of course, to ban the awful, death-by-PowerPoint approach and replace it with a more engaging and powerful presentation method. If you have an innovative company that truly understands design and creative collaboration, then you have to abandon the typical dull and lifeless PowerPoint presentation for compelling stories and conversations that are visual, simple (without being overly simplistic), and memorable. As Neumeier says, "If a business is really a decision factory, then the presentations that inform those decisions determine their quality."

What Is Design?

Design is about people creating solutions that help or improve the lives of other people—often in profound ways, but often in ways that are quite small and unnoticed. When we design, we need to be concerned with how other people interpret our design solutions and our design messages. Design is not art, although there is art in it. Artists can, more or less, follow their creative impulses and create whatever it is they want to express. But designers work in a business environment. At all times, designers need to be aware of the end user and how best to solve (or prevent) a problem from the user's point of view. Art, in and of itself, can be considered good or bad. Good art may move people; it may change their lives in some way. If so, wonderful. But good design must necessarily have an impact on people's lives, no matter how seemingly small. Good design changes things.

When most people think about design, they think about superficial things—about how things look. But design goes much deeper than that. Design is more than aesthetics, yet things that are well designed, including graphics, often have high aesthetic quality. Well-designed things look good. But does this matter? Isn't the content all that matters? In *Emotional Design: Why We Love (or Hate) Everyday Things* (Basic Books, 2004), author and designer Donald Norman suggests that good-looking designs actually work better. When it comes to physical products, such as user interfaces and displays, Norman argues that the emotional aspects of a design may often be as important to the product's ultimate success as the practical elements. Says Norman:

> *Attractive things make people feel good, which in turn makes them think more creatively...positive emotions are critical to learning, curiosity, and creative thought.*

In the case of presentation visuals, graphics must be free of errors and they must be accurate. But our visuals—like it or not—also touch our audiences at an emotional level. People make instant judgments about whether something is attractive, trustworthy, professional, too slick, and so on. This is a visceral reaction—and it matters.

14 Ways to Think Like a Designer

OK, so we know design matters. But can professionals and students outside the world of design learn from designers? Can they learn from thinking like a designer? And what of more specialized professions? Can medical doctors, scientists, researchers, and engineers benefit from learning how a graphic designer or interactive designer thinks? Is there something designers, either through their training or experience, know that we don't? I believe there is.

Following are 14 things I have learned over the years from designers. During speaking engagements throughout the world, I often put up a slide asking people to make as many sentences as they can that begin with the word "Designers…." The goal of this activity is to get people thinking about design, which is something most of us never do. This exercise also gets people in the audience talking and loosening up a bit—always a good thing. The sentences they generate range from "Designers wear black" to "Designers use creativity and analysis to solve problems" and from "Designers make things beautiful" to "Designers make messages clear," and so on.

The following 14 items are basic qualities of good design, and they provide a solid summary of the themes in my first book, *Presentation Zen: Simple Ideas on Presentation Design and Delivery* (New Riders, 2012). Regardless of your profession, you should be able to apply many of these ideas in your own work.

1. Embrace constraints.

Constraints and limitations are wonderful allies. They lead to enhanced creativity and ingenious solutions that, without constrains, might never have been discovered. In the words of T.S. Eliot, "Given total freedom the work is likely to sprawl." Constraints can be inspiring and liberating—it all depends on your point of view. There's no point in complaining about constraints such as time, money, and tools. Your problem is what it is. How can you solve it given the resources and time that you have? Often, you'll have few options and fewer choices at your disposal. Yet, as Zen scholar Steve Hagen reminds us, in life as in design, "True freedom doesn't lie in the maximization of choice, but, ironically, is most easily found in a life where there is little choice." Learn to view limitations not as annoyances but as welcome editors that force you to think creatively.

2. Practice restraint.

Anyone can add more. It takes discipline of mind and strength of will to make the hard choices about what to include and what to exclude. Self-editing is an important skill, but it's something we all struggle with. It's hard to let go of our "babies"—those ideas we've worked on for so long and have grown so attached to—and it's sometimes impossible to see that they are unnecessary. As new media designer Hillman Curtis says, "You may include things you believe to be crucial in a design, but those elements are often only crucial to you." The genius, however, is often in what you omit.

3. Know when to stop.

Hara hachi bu, which means "Eat until 80 percent full," is a Japanese idea from the culinary world. This idea can be applied to the length of meetings and presentations, and also to the amount of content and the number of elements you use to express your message. The question "How much should I include?" can only be answered by you, as you are closest to the problem. But remember that self-restraint—the kind exercised in hara hachi bu—is difficult but often leads to greater clarity. Resist the urge to pile on more "just in case."

I've used these simple slides in workshops when talking about principles of self-control and moderation, ideas we see practiced in the Zen arts. Garden images by Markuz Wernli Saito.

"In the beginner's mind there are many possibilities. In the expert's mind there are few. "

—— Shunryu Suzuki

4. Adopt the beginner's mind.

As the old saying goes, in the expert's mind there are few possibilities, but for the beginner's mind, the world is wide open. While you are an expert at what you do, try to take a step back and approach your problem the way a child does, without preconceived notions of what can and cannot be done. As an exercise in creativity, take a chance and look at a problem from a new perspective. Designers understand the need to take risks, especially during the early explorations of a problem. They are not afraid to break with convention. Good designers are open minded and comfortable with ambiguity early in the process; this is how discoveries are made.

5. Check your ego at the door.

This is not about you; it's about them. It's about your audience, customer, patient, student, etc. Look at the problem from their point of view—put yourself in their shoes. This is not easy; it takes a great deal of empathy. Empathy, an undervalued "soft skill," can be a great differentiator that sets you apart from others. It is key to truly understanding a problem, a problem that impacts others. One of the fundamental ideas about design and design thinking is that the work is not about us. It's always about solving a problem in the best interest of others.

6. Focus on the experience of the design.

It's not the thing—it's the experience of the thing. This is related to No. 4 earlier: Put yourself in the beginner's shoes. How do people interact with your solution? It's not about the features of your product or the technical superiority of your designs; it's about what it means to the users. It's about how real people interact with your design. Remember that much of design has an emotional component—sometimes this is even the largest component, although users may be unaware of this. Do not neglect the emotional aspect of your solutions.

7. Become a master storyteller.

Often it's not only the design—the solution to a problem—that is important, but the story of it. This is related to No. 5 earlier. Ditch your ego and focus on the meaning of the solution. Practice illustrating the significance of solutions, both verbally and visually. Learn to avoid slick, polished pitches, and instead take people on a short journey that explains the significance of your design. Start with the general, then zoom in on the detail. Expand the focus again to remind us of the theme or key concept, then zoom back in to illuminate more detail. The details are important and necessary, but what people remember is the story.

8. Think communication—not decoration.

Design, even graphic design, is not about aesthetics, although aesthetics are important. As a general principle, create visuals and other designs that express what is necessary. Minimize or eliminate that which is excess. As Issac Newton said, "…more is in vain, when less will serve." Every design has a central concept or message; anything that leads to confusion or distracts from your intended message is considered noise. Nonessential elements may not always be noise—this is for you to decide on a case-by-case basis. Just be sure to always keep in mind the need to eliminate clutter to make your message clear. Design is about making things clear with as much economy and simplicity as possible.

"Simplicity means the achievement of maximum effect with minimum means."
— Dr. Koichi Kawana

Image in slide from iStockphoto.com.

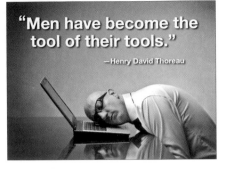

Image in slide
from iStockphoto.com.

9. Obsess about ideas—not tools.

Tools are important and necessary, but they come and go as better tools come along. Obsess, instead, about ideas. A simple pencil and sketch pad can be your most useful tools, especially in the early stages of thinking, because they are the most direct. Good advice to follow is to go analog in the beginning. The best ideas and the best designs almost always begin with a pencil and paper, a pen and a napkin, or a marker and a whiteboard. When brainstorming a solution to a problem, move away from the computer. The best presentations—including visuals for those presentations—usually start in your mind, not on your screen.

10. Clarify your intention.

Design is about choices and intentions; it is not accidental. Design is about process. Design is often systematic, although there is room for great flexibility and creativity within a system. The end user will usually not notice "the design of it." To the user, it may seem like "it just works," assuming they think about it at all. This ease-of-use or ease-of-understanding is not by accident. It's a result of your careful choices and decisions, including your deliberate choices about what to include and what to exclude.

11. Sharpen your vision and curiosity, and learn from the lessons around you.

Good designers are skilled at noticing and observing. They are able to see both the big picture and the details of the world around them. Humans are natural pattern seekers, so be mindful of this aptitude in yourself and in others. Design is a "whole brain" process. You are creative, practical, rational, analytic, empathetic, and passionate. Foster these skills in yourself and in others.

12. Simplify as much as you can—but no more.

It was Albert Einstein who said, "Everything should be made as simple as possible, but not simpler." Simplicity is our guiding principle. Simplicity means many things to many people. Scores of books have been written on the subject. For our purposes, simplicity means embracing most of the concepts discussed here to avoid the extraneous. It means making the conscious decision to cut unnecessary information and design elements. If you can do it with less, then do it with less. Yet simplicity is not only about subtraction. As MIT professor and designer John Maeda says, "Simplicity is about subtracting the obvious and adding the meaningful." You will find tools for achieving simplicity in many of the principles covered in this book, including hierarchy, unity, balance, the use of color and typography, and much more. All of these principles can help us achieve clarity of message and simplicity of design.

13. Utilize empty space.

Designers see empty space not as nothing but as a powerful something. The biggest mistake most people make is seeing empty space as something that must be filled in—as something that is wasted unless it is occupied with more elements. But it is the empty space, also called negative space or white space, that makes the positive elements of a design stand out. If you look at empty space as something to be avoided, then your designs are very likely to be cluttered. The intentional use of space does not just lead to better aesthetic qualities; it's a powerful tool for directing the eye and establishing clear design priorities. Empty space, then, is absolutely crucial for obtaining clarity in your message.

14. Learn all the "rules" and know when and why to break them.

Over the centuries, our predecessors have established guidelines, rules, and laws that you need to know. Yet, unlike other kinds of laws, it may be acceptable to break design rules at times—as long as you know why you're doing it. Basic design principles and rules are important and useful to know. That's where this simple book comes in.

Design and Presentation Zen

This is not a book about Zen, although there are references to Zen in it. In the West, we use the term Zen to represent that which feels harmonious—perhaps in a way that's hard to articulate. We just know or feel that something is great, that it works. In Japan, Zen is rarely used in everyday conversation. You hardly ever hear anyone outside the Zen arts use the word, let alone use the idea of Zen in relation to visual communication. And yet Zen has had perhaps the single biggest influence on Japanese culture and aesthetics. As a 25-year resident of Japan and a student of Japanese culture and the Zen arts, I find it impossible not to be influenced by the Zen aesthetic and all its lessons. I've found that what Zen teaches about life can also be applied to design.

While many concepts are embodied in a Zen approach, the fundamental concepts related to communication are restraint, simplicity, and naturalness. Restraint in preparation, simplicity in design, and naturalness in delivery. These are the three concepts that run through the Presentation Zen approach to communication and design—ideas I touched on in my first book, *Presentation Zen*. In this book, which focuses on design, simplicity is the underlying theme.

Simplicity

Wagasa, traditional Japanese umbrellas, are beautiful, colorful creations made by master craftspeople who use only natural ingredients such as bamboo and washi paper, just as they have for centuries (see sidebar, "Learning from Wagasa"). The kanji characters for wagasa are 和 (harmony) and 傘 (umbrella). The wagasa embodies both elegant simplicity and complexity. For the user, the wagasa is an item with both a practical function and great beauty. It seems to be the very essence of simplicity in a manmade creation—simple to use and beautiful to behold. Yet it is also complex.

The making of a wagasa requires the special knowledge and skill of not just the master wagasa craftsman but also of several master craftspeople who make many of the individual components. The design of wagasa—an inspiration for me—also serves as a subtle visual theme running through this book. The beauty of the wagasa design is a fundamental reminder that simplicity and complexity can live side by side in harmony. While simplicity is not easy for us to achieve, nor for the master wagasa craftsman, the simplicity will be greatly appreciated by the user.

The lesson here is that far from being easy, simplicity in design is actually hard to achieve. In other words, simplicity is not simple. We should not be concerned with what is easy for *us,* however, but what is easy for *them.* Thinking like a designer, our goal is to make visuals that support our message in a manner that is easiest for our audience to understand, revealing our message in the clearest way possible. Having a better understanding of key design principles will indeed make things a bit easier for us, and a lot easier for our audience. Sometimes, people create visual messages that give simplicity a bad name. They make things too simple and dumb down the message. Today, however, the more common problem is that simple things are made unnecessarily complicated with layers of obfuscation and superfluous design elements. Our goal is to create designs that are honest, true, and simple, but always simple in a way that helps the viewer understand in the clearest way possible.

Structure and freedom

Another lesson from Zen is that form (rules or structure) is necessary for freedom to exist. If you have the form, you can exercise great freedom. If you have no form, you get a situation in which everything and anything goes. It's true that we must use our own good judgment and not let the rules become a kind of bondage of their own. Nonetheless, the form is important. Many of the Zen-inspired arts such as *sumi-e* (ink and wash painting), *ikebana* (the art of flower arrangement), or *sado* (the way of tea) look beautifully simple. But the simplicity in these art forms is achieved through years of study and a deep understanding of the principles.

When it comes to visual communication, the problem for most people is that they begin to design visuals in a rather arbitrary fashion, without an understanding of the principles of graphic design. Not surprisingly, this experience is often not rewarding for the designer or the viewer. Knowing graphic design principles can lead to a more rewarding experience for everyone concerned.

Learning from Wagasa

After a ten-minute taxi ride from Kyoto station—down a narrow street and across from the quiet grounds of the Hokyoji Temple—I found myself in one of the last wagasa shops in all of Japan, and the only one in Kyoto. Wagasa are traditional Japanese umbrellas made from all-natural materials. The name of the shop is Hiyoshiya, a family business founded in the late Edo period that's been creating wagasa for more than 150 years.

Mr. Kotaro Nishibori, the shop's fifth-generation owner, is a young, award-winning master craftsman who understands the importance of learning from traditional Japanese aesthetics and design. "To respect and preserve tradition is more necessary today than ever before," says Nishibori-sensei. "Bringing old traditions and materials into the lives of the next generation is what we can do and that is the challenge that inspires me and others of my generation."

The wagasa design illustrates that what is simple is also complex. The process of creating a Japanese umbrella involves several steps that include the work of craftspeople who specialize in bamboo, woodwork, washi paper, and final adjustments. The components are natural—Japanese washi paper, bamboo, wood, linseed oil, lacquer, persimmon tannin, and tapioca glue—and the entire process from start to finish involves a few dozen difficult, time-consuming precision craft processes.

The cover of this book features a close-up photo from iStockphoto.com of a traditional Japanese umbrella—a perfect example of simplicity and beauty, yet it's rather complex in its design. The wagasa serves as a subtle reminder that we can learn a lot from studying the richness of Japanese culture, especially its culture of art and refinement. All you need to do is open your mind and think a little differently. The more high tech we become, it seems the more the past has to teach us about the fundamentals of design—and of life. It's important to preserve those fundamentals.

The precision of the final rib structure and the glued-on washi paper work together to fold away simply and elegantly. Wagasa are usually stored handle down.

Nishibori-san shows the different kinds of washi paper used in his store's designs.

Nishibori-san explains that to create the ribs of Japanese umbrellas, craftspeople split bamboo into very thin strips.

Nishibori-san "goes digital" and uses PowerPoint to explain the history of the wagasa to me in the office of his studio in Kyoto.

The Hiyoshiya shop is located in the Kamigyo-ku district of Kyoto. See their Web site in both English and Japanese: www.wagasa.com

About This Book

Many ways exist to explore the basics of graphic design. I approach the challenge by first giving you an overview of the basic components common to slide presentations: type, color, images (including video), and charts and graphs. I offer some simple solutions and considerations for using these elements to their greatest potential for effective communication. With a good understanding of these basic components, we can use them as fundamental building blocks for exploring the important design principles that follow. These components consist of using space, creating balance among the elements, and achieving harmony through unity. In this second edition of the book, I also look at the elements of storytelling and how understanding the basic structure of a story can enhance your ability to create presentations that engage your audience.

While there are examples from presentations included in each chapter, Chapter 10 contains a number of examples for you to see some of the principles in action. To bring perspectives in from other fields, I've included interviews with experts on topics such as photography and the use of color. You'll find these as sidebars that run throughout the book.

In Sum

- Design, at its most fundamental level, is about finding solutions. It is in our interest as professionals to become more knowledgeable about design in general and graphic design and visual communication in particular.

- In the case of presentation visuals, designs must be free of errors and they must be accurate. Visuals also touch our audience at an emotional level.

- Simplicity in design sounds easy, but is actually hard to achieve. The goal is to make visuals that support our message in a manner that is easiest for our audience to understand and reveals our message in the clearest way possible. Having a better understanding of key design principles will indeed make things a bit easier for us—and a lot easier for our audience.

- Form (rules or structure) is necessary for freedom to exist. If you have the form, you can exercise great freedom. If you have no form—if everything and anything goes—you often create an experience that is not rewarding for the designer or the viewer.

components

You learn the basics because
they make your work easier and
your designs better.

— John McWade,
designer and author

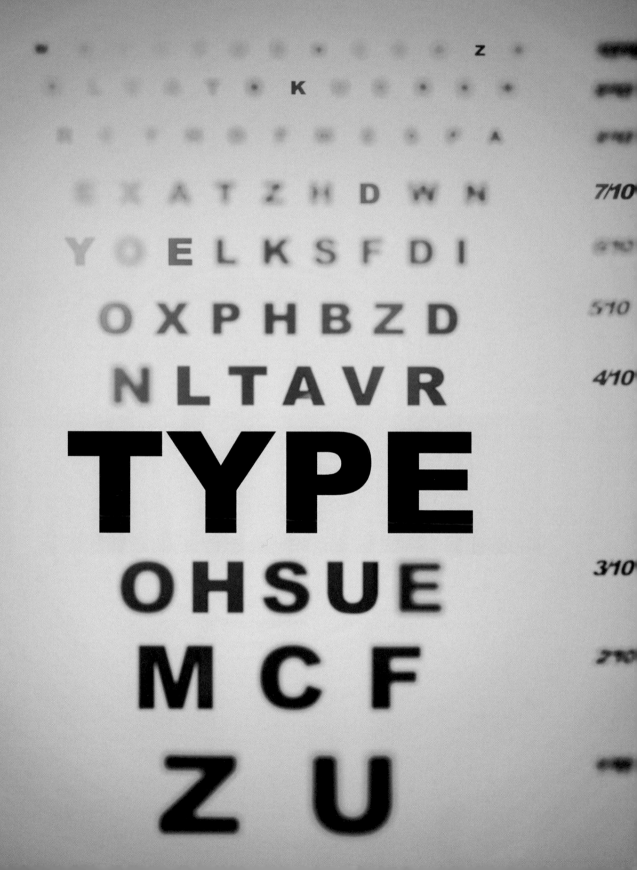

2

Presenting
with Type

Typography is often taken for granted. Like the air we breathe, the ubiquity of type in our daily lives is not something most people think about. However, once you take a closer look and begin to study the art of typography, you discover that type has both an aesthetic quality and a function: It can be as beautiful as it is useful. When you put a word into type, you have given it a visual form along with the verbal meaning. This dual nature of typography is what makes it so fascinating and so potentially powerful.

While it is not necessary for you to become an expert in typography to use type well, it's in your interest to deepen your awareness and understanding of the rich art of typography. Today, virtually everyone can name at least a few typefaces—even if their knowledge doesn't go much beyond a casual familiarity with their names. (You may know typefaces as fonts, because that is the term that word processors, email programs, and other software use for typeface. In many cases, type, typeface, and font are used interchangeably.) To many people, the typeface selected may seem like a superfluous thing, but this is incorrect. The proper choice and usage of type can go a long way toward making your visual message heard.

While audiences may view type on a slide as text to read, its shape, size, color, and texture also affect its meaning and the feelings the viewers interpret. At other times, type on a slide (or a page) is a purely visual element that can stand on its own as an effective visual, with no accompanying image.

With presentations, we are ultimately interested in using type in the most effective and harmonious way possible to create powerful, memorable visuals and clear communication. Simplicity is especially important when working with type as it is easy to unintentionally add noise and clutter through the inappropriate use of type. Most mistakes occur today because professionals outside of the design world are unfamiliar with the basics of type in general, but especially when used in a presentation environment.

Designing for the Last Row

Type must make our words clear. Audiences should not have to work hard just to decipher meaning from the letter forms. Some typefaces are more effective for reading quickly, and they are often used for billboards, posters, and slides. Other forms of type are easier on the eyes when reading longer passages of text, such as a book or journal. Because our goal as presenters is to present content and have people listen, we're not as concerned with "readability" as we are with clarity. It's difficult for people to read and listen to you at the same time anyway.

The question for us is always can they see—and read quickly with ease— the type on our slides. Clear, effective type is especially important when you consider presenting visuals in a large room where people are sitting at various distances from the screen, sometimes quite far away. Always design for the people in the last row.

Make it big!

The problem with most presentation visuals is not that the text is too big, but that it is way too small. If you need to put lots of text onscreen, you may need to rethink your presenting style. For smaller groups sitting around conference tables or in meeting rooms, projecting slides onscreen may not be the best medium for presenting deep levels of detail. In this case, you may consider a handout for portions of your talk. But for larger presentations at conferences and in classrooms and lecture halls, and so on, why not make the text large enough for instant reading while offering visual impact? This is not a gimmick. Remember, people are there to listen to you speak—and the visuals can help illustrate and back up your points—but no one is there to read a load of slides or listen to you read them.

Display screens for keynote presentations or large conference talks have more in common with billboards or road signs. The elements, including type, must be large enough to be seen and understood instantly from a distance. There is no excuse for making people squint. Make it big and make it clear.

So what's the minimum point size for slide text? This depends on how big the presentation screen is. If you cannot make out the text when viewing slides in the slideware's slide-sorter view, then your text is probably too small for everyone in your audience to read.

To cap or not to cap?

What about setting type in all uppercase? For short headlines or a single word, using all uppercase letters is acceptable and can make a powerful statement, but use this technique with restraint. For longer sentences, type set in all uppercase can be hard on our eyes (and our brains). For longer passages, all uppercase type is just too hard to read.

If the amount ot text is small, uppercase type can work.

Compare the all uppercase phrase at left to the same phrase in "sentence case" with only the first words capitalized. The text in this slide might be a little easier for the audience to read.

This slide may work for a smaller group setting, but the small type in uppercase is going to be hard for people in the back of the room to read. (Images in slides from iStockphoto.com.)

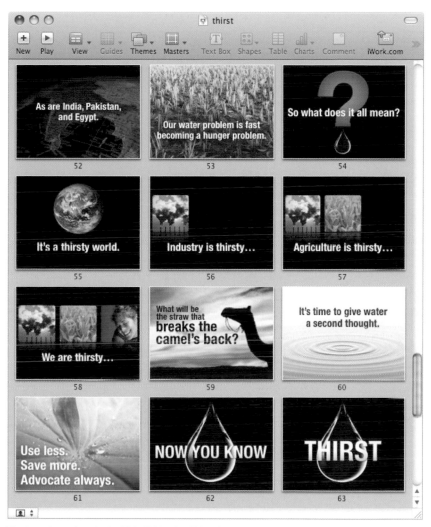

The type shown here in the Light Table view (Slide Sorter in PowerPoint) ranges in size from 72 pt. to 120 pt. (Slides by Jeff Brenman.)

Avoid clutter

As stated in the opening paragraphs of this chapter, simplicity is the key to using type effectively in your presentations. A fundamental tenet of simplicity is excluding the nonessential. Extra or decorative elements often result in visuals that feel cluttered, and the meaning of the text may be weakened as a result. You can look at four different things to eliminate clutter and simplify:

1. Look at the design of the typeface itself. Are the lines clean and the letterforms easy to read at the current size?

2. Do other elements in the slide make the type harder to read?

3. Is there simply too much text for one slide? Can you eliminate some text and retain meaning?

4. Type displayed in too many colors can also add a feeling of clutter and visual noise.

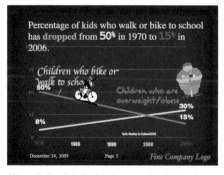

Although the data is simple, even simple trends become more difficult to absorb when too many fonts and other elements are used.

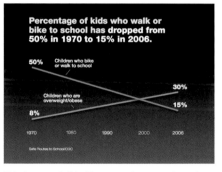

This improved slide illustrates the general trend while the presenter filled in the details. Note that if the specific numbers for each year are important, a table in a handout would work better.

Let the letters breathe

Your software is already doing a pretty good job of automatically adjusting the space between all the different letter pairs and in the vertical space between lines of type. But when you make type quite large—which you often do when working with slides—you need to pay close attention to the spacing in the text to ensure maximum legibility.

When the spacing between pairs of letters in text looks uneven, we need to manually adjust the space using something known in the typography world as *kerning*. Look carefully at the words in the slide shown here.

Some letter pairs, such as TS, require more space between them than pairs such as AW. All the gaps between letters should have the same optical space (rather than actual space). With the same optical space, the edges of some letter pairs overlap—such as AW and WA—and other letter pairs will not overlap—such as AL and WK.

Can you see the difference between these two slides? In the first slide, the "Aw" and "WA" have too much space between them. The second slide is better.

Whether you need to and can kern certain letter pairs depends on your software and the font in use. The important thing is to become more aware of the space between letters, especially when you design with large type, and make adjustments when you can. Free fonts downloaded from the Internet and low-quality fonts may have worse default spacing. If you find yourself spending a lot of time making adjustments, consider using a different font.

Let the lines breathe

As you increase the size of slide text, you might notice that the amount of vertical space between lines increases too much. The space between lines in a paragraph is known as *leading*, and too much of it—or too little of it—makes text in your slides difficult to read.

In presentation software, leading is usually set by default to around 20 percent larger than the type size. For example, if your type is set to 12 pt, the leading is usually around 14 or 15 points, which works pretty well for print documents. But when you increase the type size in slideware, the space between lines may seem too great. If you use large type in slides—for a long quote, for example—you may want to reduce the leading (called line spacing in many programs). Adjusting the space between lines is one way to make sure that related elements are near each other.

List items are considered individual paragraphs and you need to use the Space Before and Space After controls to adjust the spacing above and below a bulleted list. (If you're using PowerPoint, all these controls can be accessed by choosing Format > Line Spacing.)

In this slide on the top left, the leading value is too high as often happens automatically in slideware. It looks like there are seven elements in the slide—six type elements and an image. The lines of type in the slide at top right are too tight. It's difficult to read this text, especially for those in the audience at the back of the room. The line spacing in the slide on the bottom is much tighter but not too tight. It appears as if there are now three components on top of the background—a title, a list, and one graphic. (Images in slides from iStockphoto.com.)

In the first slide (above left) there is too much leading. Although it is legible, the line spacing is uncomfortably wide. The line spacing in the slide directly above is much better. The third slide (left) has even tighter spacing but still leaves room for the lines to breathe. Any tighter than this, though, and the descender in the letter "g" may crash into the line below it, something you generally want to avoid.

Too much spacing.

This is better. (Images in slides from iStockphoto.com.)

Type is saying things to us all the time. Typefaces express a mood, an atmosphere. They give words a certain coloring.

— Rick Poynor,
design critic and author

Choosing Your Type

When considering the type to use for presentation visuals, focus on how legible the type is when displayed onscreen and how easy it is to read shorter sections of text. Generally, a sans serif typeface is best for projected slides, but at large sizes, even a serif typeface such as Garamond is legible. When I worked at Apple, most sales presentations were formatted with Helvetica and Apple's own version of the oldstyle typeface Garamond (Apple Garamond).

The typeface you choose depends on your content and even your own personality. Although people in the audience are not consciously aware of it, the typeface says something about your content, and even about you. Use type intelligently for communicating your ideas, then look beyond the literal meaning of the words. Additional information is expressed through associations attached to the style of type. Type can set a mood. If you are tasked with using corporate or logo fonts, then let that be your guide. But there are thousands of typefaces to choose from, including many that are already installed in your computer. How do you choose which to use?

Some reliable typefaces

In *Typography Essentials* (Rockport Publishers, 2009), designer Ina Saltz identifies six necessary typefaces to have in your repertoire: Caslon, Garamond, Baskerville, Helvetica, Futura, and Gill Sans. So many typefaces are available that it can be very difficult to practice restraint, says Saltz. Not only that but the abundance of choices can be crippling for many people—they simply do not know where to begin. Too many choices often leads to hurried and arbitrary decisions about what typeface to use. So having six to ten typefaces that you understand well and use often is a good base from which to start. The six identified by Ina Saltz are excellent. I like those six plus my classic favorites: Bodoni, Univers, Rockwell, Frutiger, and Franklin Gothic.

Reliable typefaces

Baskerville	Refined, dignified, beautifully simple
Bodoni	Elegant, subjective, classic yet modern feel
Caslon	Dignified, formal, sturdy yet graceful
Franklin Gothic	Classic sans serif popular for use in large displays such as billboards
Frutiger	Sturdy, legible, simple, clean
Futura	Elegant sans serif, great personality yet understated
Garamond	Classic elegance, mature without being stuffy
Gill Sans	Sans serif with a distinct, warm, friendly personality
Helvetica	Neutral without being boring, simple, contemporary
Optima	Clean, classy, soothing, smart
Rockwell	Distinct, bold, confident, good display type

Why do some of these typefaces work so well for presentation design? And how do you choose among them? Some of the fonts in this list are serif typefaces. Serifs are the small detail at the ends of strokes within letters. (Letters without those details are called "sans serif.") Serif fonts are commonly believed to aid readability for longer sections of text because the serifs lead your eye from one character and one word to the next. Some serif fonts, however, are good choices for slide presentations as well. Baskerville, Bodoni, Caslon, Frutiger, Garamond, and Rockwell all work well for slides. The sans serif fonts in the list include Franklin Gothic, Frutiger, Futura, Gill Sans, Helvetica, and Optima.

It's generally accepted that sans serif fonts work better on computer screens as they lack the counter strokes and thin lines of the serif typefaces that can be hard to read at low resolutions. Sans serif type grew out of the German Bauhaus movement in the early 1900s, influencing type design toward a cleaner, more functional and stripped-down look. Sans serif became the preferred typeface style for billboards and a great deal of the signage around us. I recommend sans serif typefaces for use in presentations, too. Sans serif typefaces look great at large sizes and pop out well on projection screens, making them extremely legible.

Compare the same text in each of the reliable typefaces in slide format. The titles and bullets are at the same point size so you can see that the actual size onscreen depends a lot on the typeface that you use. You can see an example of Gill Sans on page 44.

All in the family

A type family consists of a group of fonts—in myriad sizes and weights—designed with a consistent style. For example, Helvetica Neue consists of a huge type family that includes several different weights (such as lights and bolds), italics, and condensed variations. Usually, you need to purchase commercial fonts to get fonts with large families, but some may already be installed on your system. Helvetica Neue comes preinstalled on most recent versions of the Mac OS in Light, Light Italic, Ultra-light, Ultra-light Italic, Italic, Regular, Bold, Bold Italic, Condensed Bold, and Condensed Black.

Consider choosing a typeface for your presentation that contains several different weights within the same type family. This gives you flexibility while at the same time making it easier to keep harmony among the fonts you choose. These different weights and styles are more than you'd ever use in one presentation. Choose two or three that have good contrast and work well together. Because they are all from the same type family, you can get away with using quite a variety of weights—if you have a reason. Using typefaces from the same font family for a project is one way to shoot for harmony, but remember to use different weights and sizes to establish hierarchy, add emphasis, and create visual interest. Using type from the same family does not at all mean the design will be dull.

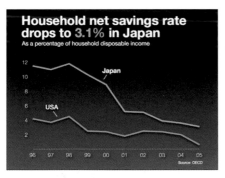

This slides uses four different weights but all are from the same family (Helvetica Neue).

Creating Harmony

When you design with type, the goal is to create harmonious relationships. For a subdued look, you might use typefaces of similar weight and style within the same family and not vary the sizes much. For a more dynamic but still harmonious look, you can combine typefaces that are clearly different and vary the weight and style. The size and location of the type impacts the relationship as well. Try mixing type from the same font family or mixing type from two families such as a classic serif and a clean, bold sans serif.

How many typefaces to use

A common concern is how many different typefaces to use in one design (or in our case, in one deck of slides). A good rule of thumb is one or two (or sometimes three). The different sizes and weights create hierarchy naturally, so anything more than two different typefaces is usually not necessary. You can use more than two, but just be clear that you have a good reason for doing so.

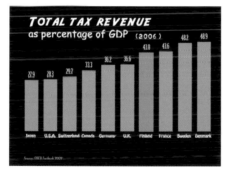

This slide uses six different typefaces. Yuck.

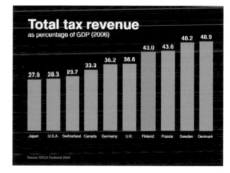

Helvetica in Bold and Regular—that's it.

Be careful not to use two (or more) different typefaces that are similar but not the same. Using Gill Sans and Optima in the same slide is a good example of a subtle clash. Both typefaces look sort of similar in that they are sans serifs with a calligraphic look and variations between the thick and thin parts of their letterforms. They are both great on their own, but used together they are the typographic equivalent of wearing a navy blazer with pants that are almost—but not quite—the same color.

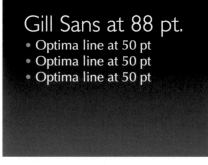

Title is set in Gill Sans Light, bullets in Optima. They are different, but not different enough.

Title is set in Gill Sans, bullets in Gill Sans Light. They are different enough but also more harmonious as they are from the same type family.

This type of problem can even occur with type from the same family used at slight variations in size. For example, if one line is 48 points and another line is 45 points, the slight difference in size looks accidental. Are they supposed to be different? If so, what does the difference mean? You can prevent confusion by making sure that the type for various levels of meaning (heads, subheads, and body text) are markedly different in size, weight, style, family, and so forth.

Type that sets a tone

Classic typefaces categorized as serif or sans serif—in all their many forms— can certainly be used to evoke feelings beyond the mere meaning of the words. For example, a large, bold version of a classic sans serif may suggest power, assertiveness, or confidence, whereas the same type in a smaller and lighter version will be more subtle and suggest a quieter confidence, humility, or calm. Some typefaces call more attention to themselves than others. While the form of a simple typeface such as Helvetica is essentially neutral, other typefaces call great attention to their forms. Depending on your content, an offbeat, overly formal, or otherwise unusual typeface can be very effective at creating a certain mood (see page 55 for an example). It is important, however, to use discretion when using typefaces with pronounced personalities. Be careful, for example, to not use a typeface that is incongruous with the meaning of the words or the desired effect.

Text placement on slides

When you insert a new text box in slideware, the type you enter is horizontal. This is obviously a good default choice, but you may consider placing text at angles or in unconventional locations (depending on the subject and audience). Unusual placement from time to time adds a dynamic dimension.

Most people never think to use a rotated effect for text, yet it is an effective technique when done with discretion. Type placed at an angle will get attention if all the other elements—including other type—have perfectly horizontal and vertical lines. Professional graphic designers often use rotated type because it pops out: It may imply motion, informality, nonconformity, power, change, and so on. Type also can be rotated at a subtle angle that allows for the type to fit more harmoniously with the content of the image.

Type can be rotated so it angles upward or downward, depending on the design or mood you're trying to achieve. (Images in slides from iStockphoto.com.)

In Defense of Helvetica

Helvetica was designed by Max Miedinger and Eduard Hoffmann in the late 1950s in Münchenstein, Switzerland. The original name, Neue Haas Grotesk, was later changed to Helvetica, the Latin word for Switzerland. Many in the design world think that Helvetica is overused and boring. Others are enamored with it and use virtually nothing else. Helvetica gets a bad rap in part because it does not have a strong personality of its own. Some would say it has no personality. While Helvetica is certainly ubiquitous, ubiquity is not always a bad thing. The ubiquity may just be a sign that it's working well—that it's a part of a civilized society.

Personally, I like Helvetica. I don't think of the typeface as dull or boring. I think of it as neutral—not in a colorless, noncommittal way, but in a way that's helpful and intentional. There is a sort of Zen in the way Helvetica is perfectly, beautifully bland (and yet, not bland).

To me, Helvetica is to typography like Japanese white rice is to traditional Japanese cuisine. That is, on its own it may seem pretty bland. While I love Japanese rice with any traditional Japanese meal, a bowl of white rice by itself would be quite boring and not very satisfying. As a balanced complement to all the other elements in a washoku meal, the rice is truly a delicious and harmonious amplifier of the entire culinary experience. Helvetica is a bit like this—the typeface is a great complement to other design elements on the page, poster, or slide. Helvetica provides clarity without drawing attention to its own form. Because Helvetica is neutral and lacks a strong personality, you could say its clean lines go well with many elements, such as images, especially those with lots of detail where the text needs to pop out without stealing the show.

I understand why some find Helvetica bland and why others find it beautiful. Helvetica—although not new—is actually refreshing in its simplicity and neutrality. It allows the meaning of the words themselves, in the context of various designs, to express themselves with a feeling of trustworthiness and reliability.

While Helvetica works well in designs with many elements—such as those found in large posters or projected screens, and inside images that are quite busy or otherwise dynamic—the dignified yet humble typeface also works in isolation at small sizes surrounded by big portions of empty space. Helvetica also works well on its own at very large sizes. Helvetica may be neutral, but in a proper context it's not bland; in fact, it's quite beautiful.

> *Helvetica was a real step from the 19th century typeface. We were impressed by that because it was more neutral, and neutralism was a word that we loved. It should be neutral. It shouldn't have a meaning in itself. The meaning is in the content of the text and not in the typeface.*
>
> — *Wim Crouwel, in the documentary* Helvetica

This slide showcases Helvetica type in different sizes and weights. (Image from iStockphoto.com.)

Complementing Images with Text for Stronger Messages

Images can improve recognition and recall, and images combined with text can make for an even stronger message—as long as the text and images reinforce the same message. Photographs are powerful on their own and can be used to form their own narrative, but when we combine text with photos, we alter the meaning just a bit. The placement, style, and meaning of the text within the picture all have a part in guiding the viewer's interpretation of the image. This goes both ways, of course. An image can also change the meaning of text. Notice in the simple examples that follow how the meaning changes. The photograph alone may have several different meanings depending on your interpretation; once we add text, the message changes.

Notice how the meaning changes when text is added to the slides above. (Image in slides from iStockphoto.com.)

Images always impact the narrative, sometimes in big ways but often in very small ways. These six slides contain the same text. Ask yourself how the meaning of the text subtly changes with each different image. (Images in slides from iStockphoto.com.)

Placing text on images

Placing text over a dynamic image with little empty space always poses legibility problems. One way to deal with this is to use boxes of solid or transparent color between the image and the text to separate the text from the image and bring it forward. There are many methods for doing this, so be sure to use a similar technique throughout the presentation for a unified look. The following slide sample contains a colorful, high-contrast photo of a street in Tokyo. It would be difficult for text to pop out from this busy scene without a little help.

The first slide in this series is the original. The text pops out a bit because the background image is slightly blurry in that area. The four slides that follow contain transparent boxes between the image and the text, which makes the type even easier to see. (Image in slides from iStockphoto.com.)

Creating Bilingual Slides

Increasingly, presenters are facing bilingual audiences. For example, foreign nationals in Japan often make presentations in English to an audience that is a mix of native English speakers and native Japanese speakers. Many Japanese audience members say they appreciate having both Japanese and English text appear onscreen at the same time.

Combining languages on a slide can be effective as long as the text is in different sizes. One language needs to be visually subordinate to the other. If I am presenting in Japanese, then the Japanese text is larger than the English text (but in a way that creates a harmonious fit). If I speak in English, the English is larger. If text from both languages is the same size, it creates visual discord as the type elements compete with each other for attention. The technique of placing text from one language in a clearly dominant position is commonly used in signage for public transportation and in advertising.

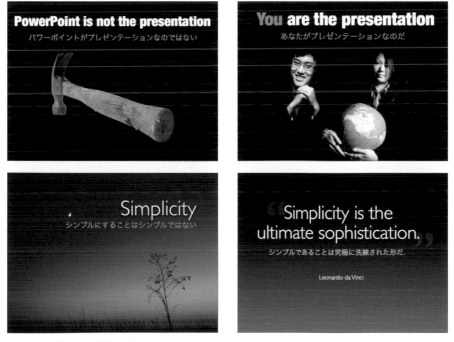

Images in slides from iStockphoto.com.

David S. Rose

Technology entrepreneur, world-class presenter

www.rose.vc

Known as The Pitch Coach and "The father of angel investing in New York," David S. Rose gives some priceless advice for those making presentations to VCs and Angels for investments.

Tips on design and delivery when the stakes are high

The primary hallmark of an entrepreneurial fundraising pitch as opposed to other types of presentations is that the most important factor by far is *you.* Investors are going to spend the entire session attempting to determine if *you* are the person behind whom they should invest their money. How *you* come across personally is often more important than everything else combined, including your business plan, industry, and financial projections. This means that fundraising pitches *must* be given by the CEO and no one else. The top ten characteristics that investors will be looking to find in you during your presentation are integrity, passion, experience (in starting a business), knowledge, skill (in functional operating areas), leadership, commitment, vision, realism, and coachability.

Presentation flow

The single most important thing in sequencing a presentation is that everything must flow logically from beginning to end, and require no prior knowledge on the part of the audience. You do not want the audience to have to "think" at all, which means you need to answer every potential question at exactly the right place, just before the audience would think to ask it. It sounds easy, but 99% of presentations don't do it.

The opening

The world's greatest presentation trainers, such as Granville Toogood (*The Articulate Executive*) and Jerry Weissman (*Presenting to Win*), all agree that the presenter has between 30 and 60 seconds to grab the attention of the audience. To do this, start with nothing on the screen but your company logo, your name, and your title. Then, begin with something dramatic and memorable that will have the audience wanting to follow along with you for the rest of the presentation. This opening can be a personal anecdote, an unusual number, a historic progression, a counterintuitive fact, whatever is appropriate. Virtually anything that will start the presentation with a bang and set the mood for the remainder of the pitch is desirable.

Context setting

It is crucial that after the opening, the presenter immediately set the context for the rest of the presentation. This should not be the agenda for the presentation, but rather (at least for a venture fundraising pitch) an extraordinarily concise explanation of what the heck the company does: "We manufacture and sell buggy whips"; "We operate a search engine that finds anything on the Internet"; whatever.

Consider this to be the picture on the outside of a jigsaw puzzle box—the element that gives the audience the overall picture into which they can then fit each piece as you deliver it.

Sequence

The slide/topic sequence for a fundraising pitch is pretty straightforward and should only be deviated from after careful consideration. It should look like this:

Company Logo [during the opening]
Business Overview [the context setter]
Management Team
Market/Pain Points
Product [including photos or screen shots]
Business Model
Customers [current and projected]
Strategic Relationships [if any]
Competition
Barriers to Entry
Financial Overview
Capital, Valuation, and Use of Proceeds
Review (Logo/Image)

Validators

Throughout the presentation, subject material should be liberally surrounded by "validators" that lend outside credence to the claims the presenter is making. These can range from the rock solid ("IBM, a repeat customer, has already paid us $10 million for our widgets and says we're the best they've ever seen"), to the usual ("Gartner projects a tenfold increase in the buggy whip market over the next five years"), to something as simple as laying out a competitive landscape that includes brand names the audience has heard of ("McDonald's sells standardized hamburgers around the world; we sell custom burgers in Tokyo").

Things to avoid at all costs

Things the audience knows are not true
Things the audience doesn't understand
Things that make the audience "think"
Internal inconsistencies
Typos, errors, general unpreparedness

Slide design

Less is more (and even less is even more). None of the greatest speakers throughout history ever used PowerPoint. By definition any time the audience is looking at the screen, they are not looking at you. (Remember, *you* are the most important thing in the presentation.) Humans are completely incapable of reading and comprehending text on a screen and listening to a speaker at the same time. Therefore, lots of text (almost *any* text!), and long, complete sentences are bad, Bad, BAD.

David S. Rose

The leave-behind

Never, ever hand out copies of your slides after your presentation, and certainly not before your presentation. That is the kiss of death. By definition, since slides are "speaker support" material, they are there in support of the speaker—that is, you. Therefore, slides should be completely incapable of standing by themselves and are useless to give to your audience as they will simply be guaranteed to be a distraction during your talk. The flip side of this is that if the slides *can* stand by themselves, why the heck are you up there in front of them? Just hand out the slides and sit down! Instead, prepare a leave-behind deck that is *different* from (and substantially more complete than) the presentation you actually give (but that follows the same general structure). This should be left behind *after* you finish.

Builds

People are only capable of absorbing a very small amount of material at a time. Therefore, it is counterproductive to throw up a slide with lots of text or complicated diagrams. Each change on the screen should relate to one simple new thought that should be expanded and explained by the presenter. As such, I am a great fan of "builds," in which text or a diagram is built in front of the audience over several minutes. Since each advance is effectively a new slide, it is possible to slowly and simply build up to a comprehensive dénouement without losing your audience along the way. I have done builds with 15 or more components, which when delivered properly, can take upward of 15 minutes to run through but never result in flagging audience attention.

Delivery

Here's a key concept that is completely counter-intuitive, but unbelievably powerful: "Say it, *then* show it," rather than "Show it, *then* say it." The vast majority of presenters put up a slide on the screen, glance at it, and then read it out loud to the audience. This is completely and disastrously wrong. The right way (but difficult until you've practiced enough to get comfortable with it) is to start talking about the next point while you are still on the previous slide, and only then bring up the new slide. This puts you in command of the presentation, and not the other way around. It trains the audience to expect that all new and important information is coming from you rather than from a slide deck.

Prompting

Aside from complete familiarity with your subject matter (which can only come from constant practicing), presenters using computer-based slides should always take advantage of the preview/prompting capability of their software. PowerPoint users have Presenter Tools, Keynote users have Presenter's Dashboard, and Adobe users have Ovation software, which runs PowerPoint presentations in a powerful prompting interface. These software features help prevent you from having to turn your head to the screen and from forgetting what is on the next slide.

I created these slides for one of my business classes based entirely on a deck that David S. Rose used in his own seminars. The irregularity of the type is built into the font, giving it a more analog, informal, retro feel. (Images in slides from iStockphoto.com.)

The Little Things Matter

Getting the little things right is what sets professionals apart from amateurs. Because you know your content and you know what you are talking about, don't let the type on screen suggest otherwise. I won't get into the minutia of good grammar and punctuation here, but if you care enough about getting your point across to your audience in a professional way, then avoiding common typographic and punctuation errors is important. A few simple things you can do to clean up the text in your slides follow.

Use proper apostrophes and quotation marks

Sometimes a mistake occurs so regularly that many people don't even notice it. One such error is the backward apostrophe. This is admittedly a small thing, but it's one of those little things we need to get right. Believe it or not, there is an entire Web site dedicated to showcasing apostrophe abuse on a near daily basis (www.apostropheabuse.com). In the examples, many of the signs contain words with unnecessary or backward apostrophes.

This photo, which I shot in Nagoya recently, shows some very creative apostrophe abuse. No apostrophe is needed in this case, but if you're going to use it, you might as well put it on the correct side of the year.

Other issues with apostrophes and quotation marks are related to typography:

- **The "dumb" apostrophe.** Most people know where an apostrophe goes, but they often use the wrong one at the beginning of words such as 'til for 'til. Your software may deduce that you are starting a quotation and give you an open single quotation mark. To get a proper apostrophe for these cases, you may need to use a keyboard command. Press Shift + Option +] (Mac) or Alt + 0146 (Windows) to get the single closed quotation mark (apostrophe).

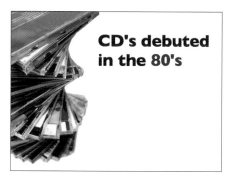

CD's debuted in the 80's

This is common, but incorrect.

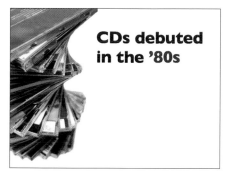

CDs debuted in the '80s

This is better.

Back in the 80's

Again, this is common, but incorrect.

Back in the '80s

Apostrophe is in the right place, but it is backwards (i.e., it's an open quotation mark).

Back in the '80s

Almost, but this is a "dumb" apostrophe.

Back in the '80s

This is correct.

- **Use proper quotation marks.** Using straight quotes rather than curly (or smart) quotes irks many designers. In most software applications, straight quotes are converted to curly quotes as you type or when you import text. If that doesn't happen, go to the preferences and turn on the Use Smart Quotes feature to include them in your work. This doesn't guarantee you will not see dumb quotes pop up once in awhile. If you copy and paste a quotation from a Web site or an email that contains quotation marks, dumb quotes may appear in your text (if they appeared in the original text).

- **Don't use curly quotation marks for inches and feet.** It's just as bad to use curly quotes when you need straight ones. When presenting the words "inches" or "feet" as a quote mark, use the prime mark for those. If the font you're using doesn't have a prime or double prime mark, insert the straight quotation mark and italicize it.

Polish up your quotes

If you look at pull quotes in magazines and newspapers or on the evening news—which are interesting excerpts from a story or interview that are pulled from the story to draw readers and viewers in—you'll notice that the opening quotation mark hangs outside the text box. This is called "hanging the punctuation" and creates a nice clean line and a stronger, more professional look. You can hang punctuation in slideware by making a new text box for that quote mark and moving it to hang outside of the quoted material

Quotation marks at the same size as the type projected onscreen can be hard to see, so consider increasing the size of the quotation marks. Making the quotation marks larger is not just a stylistic consideration, it also serves to draw people's eyes into the screen and makes it very clear that the text is a quote. Notice the quotes in the two slides at the top of the next page.

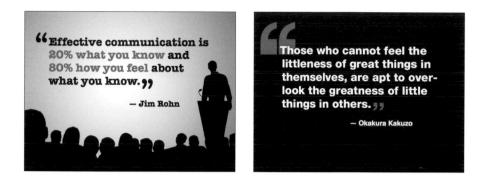

Give pause with an em dash

You may find yourself adding hyphens and dashes to slide text and it's easy to get the rules confused.

- Use hyphens (-) to join compound words, such as in "right-hand man."
- Use an en dash (–) to show a range of numbers such as "ages 8–10."
- Use em dash (—) for an abrupt pause or change in thought or speech within a sentence.

Make sure to use the correct character for the em dash. A double hyphen (--) is not the same and reflects poorly on your work if you use it. There should be no space between your text and the em dash either. Also, if you can avoid it, don't hyphenate text in slides. Hyphenation is used to copyfit long lines of text, but shouldn't be necessary for the amount of text that appears on slides.

BEFORE

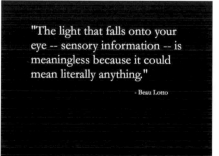

AFTER ▼

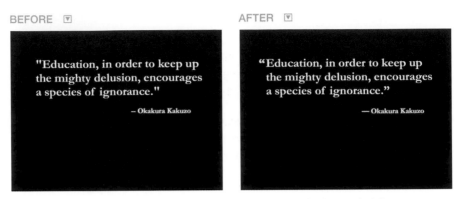

The "after" slides above and on the previous page use "smart" quotes that hang to the left, allowing the letters to form a nice even vertical line.

Emphasize with italics or bold

If you want to emphasize type on a slide, consider changing the type to bold or italics, increasing the size, or changing the color. Generally, you should avoid underlining text as it looks amateurish. If you do want to underline text, create a line using the drawing tools in your slideware. The advantage of drawing a line versus underlining text is that you can adjust the thickness of the line and keep the line from crossing over the descenders in your type.

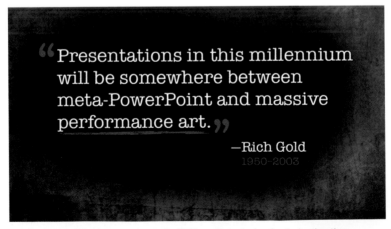

The line in the slide above was created with the software's drawing tool rather than selecting "underline text," which would have created a thin line through the bottom of the P.

In Sum

- Clear, effective type is especially important when presenting visuals in large rooms where people are sitting at various distances from the screen, sometimes quite far away. Always design for the last row.

- Your typeface choice depends on your content and even your own personality. Although people in the audience are not consciously aware of it, your selection of typeface says something about your content and even about you.

- You can achieve harmony using type in many ways. Try mixing type from the same font family or mixing type from two families such as a classic serif and a clean, bold sans serif. Add images to text to reinforce your message. Put your text in unconventional places on the slide. But always keep simplicity in mind.

- Since you know your content well, don't let the type onscreen suggest otherwise. Learn the basics of proper punctuation and check your spelling. A misstep here instantly makes you lose credibility.

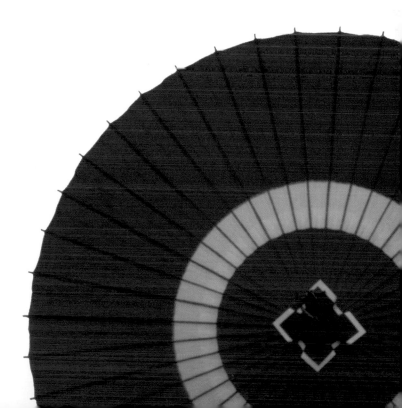

Communicating
with Color

Color is one of the most powerful visual stimuli there is. It gets our attention and affects us at an emotional level whether we are aware of it or not. Color can be used to get attention, to direct the eye, to categorize, to organize, to create unity, to evoke emotions, or to set a mood. In the world of presentations, colors are experienced as direct light illuminating from a screen or monitor (as opposed to colors on the printed page, which are seen as reflected light). We see colors with our eyes, but we perceive colors in our minds. Often we are not conscious of the perception, but its impact can be profound. The human eye can distinguish millions of colors and modern technology can produce nearly as many. While it is possible for us to design slides with a virtually unlimited color palette using today's software tools, it is important to remember that restraint and simplicity are our guiding principles.

Lessons from Sumi-e

Sumi-e (墨絵), the ancient art of Japanese brush painting, provides a powerful lesson concerning the use of color, communication, and restraint. Transported to Japan from China, sumi-e is deeply rooted in Zen, embodying many tenets of the Zen aesthetic, including simplicity and a focus on maximum effect with minimum means. In sumi-e, great works are achieved with only black ink on washi (rice paper) or silk scrolls. Using the black ink to achieve several variations of tones shows that powerful visual messages can be created with a single color in the form of different shades and tints. Sumi-e, like the Zen arts in general, embodies the maxim to never use more when less will do.

In sumi-e, a combination of empty space and monochromatic strokes that range from the extremely light gray to black express a great deal. When the work is complete, a red seal is placed in the composition in such a way that it contributes to the balance of the picture. (Actually, it's more of a reddish flesh tone called *shuniku*.) Of course, red pops out in a sea of black, gray, and the white empty space, and draws much attention to itself. In sumi-e paintings, the stamp is small and stands out in a harmonious way that serves to anchor the flow of the composition. The lesson here is clear: Using a few carefully selected and positioned colors is more effective than many colors indiscriminately placed.

Nōtan (濃淡) is a Japanese concept describing the use of light and dark aspects of a design in a balanced and harmonious way. Whether you use many colors or just shades of gray in your design work, the creation of light and dark elements is fundamental to its clarity. Imagine, for example, a colorful painting that maintains much of its clarity even in very low-light conditions. The careful use of light and dark in the composition contributes to the picture's interest and expressiveness, even when the hues become nearly imperceptible. Although the sumi (ink) is black, the artist can use techniques to create many shades of gray or many "colors." This use of color and arrangement of light and dark is effective for creating depth and movement in a composition. The lesson from sumi-e regarding color is simple: You can achieve more with less.

Express the Essence with Less

The objective of sumi-e is not to re-create a subject to look perfectly like the original. The objective is to capture and express the subject's essence. This is achieved not with more but with less. Therefore, useless details are omitted and every brush stroke has meaning and purpose. The minimum number of strokes or lines is used to convey the meaning. Each brush stroke is meaningful and has a purpose. There is no dabbling or going back to make corrections. The ink is indelible and the artist has one chance to get it right. The strokes themselves are said to serve as a good metaphor for life itself. That is, there is no moment except for *this* moment. You can't go back—there is only now.

Sumi-e is another example of an art that embodies simplicity and yet is, in practice, complex and takes a lifetime to master. This aspect of sumi-e is also a metaphor for life: One never truly masters the art of life or achieves perfection. The pursuit of perfection is the journey, and the journey is what it's all about.

Eight key lessons from sumi-e:

1. You can express more with less.
2. Never use more (color) when less will do.
3. Careful use of light and dark is important for creating clarity and contrast.
4. Use color with a clear purpose and informed intent.
5. Clear contrast, visual suggestion, and subtlety can exist harmoniously in one composition.
6. Omit useless details to expose the essence.
7. In all things: balance, clarity, harmony, and simplicity.
8. What looks easy is hard (but worth it).

Sumi-e painting by Kathleen Scott, Kansai Gaidai University, Osaka, Japan.

Creating Harmony with Color

As with everything else in design, we choose colors for a reason. A good rule of thumb for using color is to keep it simple. The greater the variety of color and color treatments in a design, the more complex managing this color in an effective, harmonious way becomes. Always remind yourself what your intention is when using color. Is it to emphasize or deemphasize? Is it to create a subtle—or not-so-subtle—theme across the presentation? Is it to help create flow and hierarchy, enhancing the viewers' understanding? Are you just trying to get an emotional response from the viewer? You have many things to think about with color usage.

Most people have a basic understanding of color, but many people lack the vocabulary for talking about color—particularly talking about what aspects work and which ones do not. Although the length of this book does not allow for a deep or technical exploration of color, understanding the basics and the differences between hue, value, and saturation are important and will help you look at the graphics around you in a different way. Learning the fundamental terms helps you work with color better and effectively incorporate it into your presentations.

Identify hues

Hue is the true or pure color, independent of its value and saturation. Hue is the identity of the color. The hue is what we describe when we say a color is orange, orange-red, green, or yellow-green, and so on. Think of the hue as the position the color occupies on the color wheel. The color wheel is a circular representation of hue.

The artist's color wheel has been used for centuries. While we use the RGB color scheme with its red, green, and blue primaries in the digital world of presentations, it is still helpful to be familiar with the basic color wheel. In the simple color wheel here, you can see 12 hues—three primary, three secondary, and six tertiary colors—that form the basic hues. The 12 basic hues in the color wheel actually form a continuous blend resulting in thousands of different possible hues (although most people can only name perhaps 12 to 20 different hues).

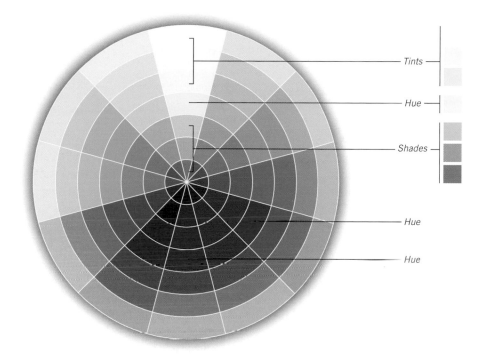

Tints

Hue

Shades

Hue

Hue

In this variation of the basic color wheel, you can find the hues, or pure color, four steps from the outside (or from the inside). As you move out you get a higher percentage of white added to the hue (tint). As you move toward the inside you have more black added (shade).

PowerPoint, Keynote, and other applications use color wheels that are loosely derived from the traditional color wheel. Pure hues are on the outermost section of the color wheel in slideware. As you move your cursor around the wheel, you can select from a virtually unlimited array of hues. You can move the dot in the wheel toward the center to get a lighter tint, or use the slider on the right of the wheel to get a darker shade of the hue. The color picker shown here is from the Mac; the custom color tools on the PC work in a similar way, giving you the ability to adjust the hue, saturation, and value.

See the value

Value (also referred to as luminance or tone) is independent of hue and refers to the relative light or dark character of the color. If you change a color image to black and white, you remove its hue but retain its tonal qualities. When you adjust the *tint*, you are adding more white to the hue, thereby making it a lighter value. When you adjust the *shade*, you are adding more black to the hue, making it a darker value.

In the early days of graphic design, knowledge of color was not as important as it is today. Then, it was more important to understand shading and how to achieve clarity with only black, white, and gray because color was a luxury not all could afford. Yet just by using different tints and shades, artists and designers could achieve clear, visually rich designs.

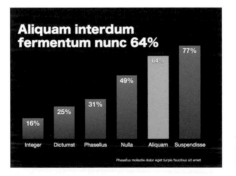

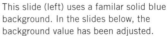

This slide (left) uses a familar solid blue background. In the slides below, the background value has been adjusted.

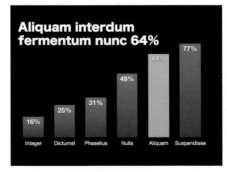

Background color is a darker shade of the original.

Background color is a lighter tint of the original.

How well color elements work in a design depends in part on the lightness or darkness of your background. Shades pop out well against white backgrounds, and tints do well against very dark backgrounds. Use caution when using backgrounds that are closer to midtones, however. How well do the shades and tints in the examples shown here pop out?

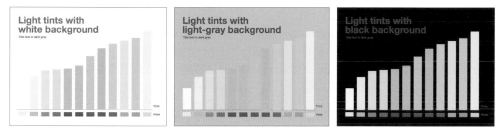

The tints of the columns in this mock bar chart are the same in each slide, but notice how the luminance varies depending on the background. Light tints stand out better on dark backgrounds.

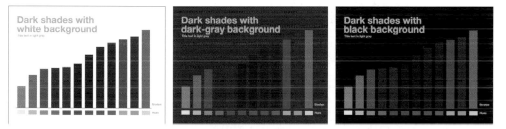

The shades in these bar charts are the same in each slide as well. All the columns pop out well on a white background, but on darker backgrounds some shades do better than others.

The first slide here is not bad, but how could you improve the other two versions to make the type stand out more?

Saturate the color

Saturation (also called chroma) is the relative purity of the hue, or its relative brightness or dullness. Saturation refers to the depth or intensity of the hue (color). Higher-saturated hues have a richness about them and stand out well. A weaker version of a hue gets closer to neutral gray. It's easiest to illustrate saturation by looking at examples from photography.

The original image (far left) has a relatively high level of saturation. Moving toward the right, each image has progressively less saturation than the original. (Image from iStockphoto.com.)

In the following sample, I took the same slide with the blue background and reduced the saturation, though the hue remains the same. Rather than becoming merely darker—as it would if you added black—the color now approaches gray.

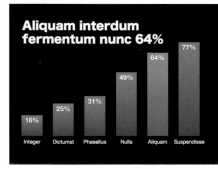

The original, simple blue background.

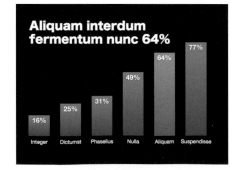

The same slide with the saturation of the background color reduced.

This slide includes a high-impact image with good levels of saturation and intensity.

The same slide with a desaturated image.

Here, the image was completely desaturated except for the snowboarder's jacket.

All the color has been removed from the image. Now only the text at the top is in color.
(Image in slides from iStockphoto.com.)

What is the color of the wind?

— Zen koan

Simple Color Combinations

Presenters can improve many visuals by simply using one of three basic color combinations based on the color wheel: monochromatic, analogous, and complementary. A fourth combination that I like is simply using an achromatic scheme (shades of black and white only) with a single hue for emphasis.

Monochromatic

Analogous

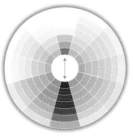
Complementary

Monochromatic schemes

A monochromatic color scheme features only one color, or hue, but in various shades and tints or at different levels of saturation. This is a very effective way to achieve harmony since using the same hue gives your slides a unified, professional look.

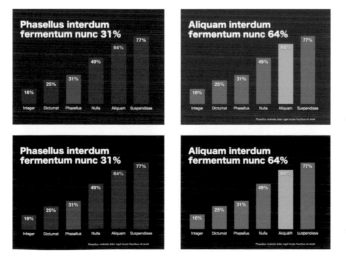

Each slide uses only one hue (plus white) in three different shades or tints.

The same simple charts with black backgrounds instead.

Analogous relationships

When you choose hues that are next to each other on the wheel, the relationship is called analogous. Starting off with analogous colors for slide elements is a very effective yet underutilized method of choosing a color scheme and a good way to achieve harmonious combinations. If you require one or more of the colors to significantly pop out (to stress a key point in your argument, for example), you may need to adjust the value or saturation levels.

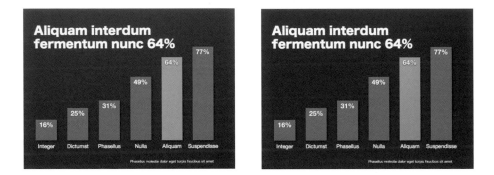

Complementary colors

Complementary colors are basically opposites, and they sit directly across from each other on the color wheel. Because they are so different, they tend to work well together. However, complementary colors are often too strong together, so you may want to adjust the tints, shades, or saturation of one or both hues to achieve a combination that is more harmonious but still offers good contrast.

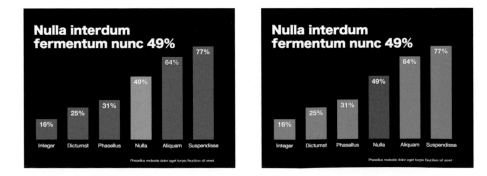

Achromatic (+1) themes

An achromatic color theme has no hues—only black, white, and shades of gray. But as we learned from the art of sumi-e, you can achieve a great deal with only black and white. One advantage of using an achromatic scheme is that you can imagine how an individual who is colorblind may see your visuals. When using color, it's very important to make sure there are clear differences in value or saturation, not simply differences in hue. One technique is something I call "achromatic +1," which simply means using an achromatic theme that includes black-and-white photography or illustrations along with only one hue. The hue is used for emphasis and may also serve as an element that repeats and adds unity to the slides.

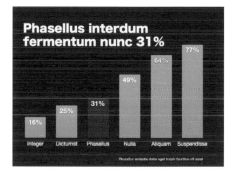 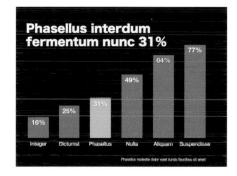

Charts use only one hue for emphasis.

Black-and-white photography with only a single element repeated in red at times throughout the presentation. (Images in slides from iStockphoto.com.)

Maureen C. Stone

Designer, scientist, teacher, author of *A Field Guide to Digital Color,* founder of StoneSoup Consulting, and adjunct professor at the Simon Fraser University School of Interactive Arts and Technology

www.stonesc.com

Color and visualization expert Maureen Stone explains how understanding color and its function can help you avoid color chaos.

Using color with purpose for functional and beautiful results

Functional color is designed for a purpose— color whose aesthetics are linked to its application or use, such as color used in a presentation or an illustration. We've all seen slides, Web pages, diagrams, and illustrations (especially computer-generated ones) with colors that are too bright, too dark, or applied so lavishly the result could be called "color chaos." Good functional color design eliminates these problems with the use of easy-to-read colors that enhance, creating a result that is both informative and aesthetically pleasing.

Color as identity

Color is the fundamental way we identify objects in the world. Our visual system is designed to instantly recognize different colors, especially those that stand out from their backgrounds like ripe fruit on a tree. This ability is not learned, but occurs "preattentively," literally, before thought.

Consider this National Park Service map of Point Reyes and its surrounding area. Like most well-designed maps, it is an excellent example of functional color. Color is used systematically to label the different regions (water, land, parkland) and to indicate the different types of roads. Using color to label and identify is

its most powerful function, and should reflect a meaningful vocabulary. In the map, the colors are chosen according to simple, well-established conventions: blue for water, green for parks, red for highways.

Color contrast

Differences in color, called *contrast*, are the fundamental way we interpret the world. Artists and vision scientists describe colors in terms of hue (red, blue, purple, etc.) and lightness, plus a third dimension variously called saturation, chroma, or "colorfulness." Differences in hue create labels. Differences in lightness define shape. Attention is drawn first to regions of high contrast.

The red roads contrast in both hue and lightness with the light-colored backgrounds. The major highways are outlined in black, which makes the color look darker and increases the contrast. The network of red highways creates the foremost visual layer in this map, as this map is designed for drivers. The roads are labeled in black, which optimizes contrast and readability.

The text that labels features in the light blue water is a slightly darker, more saturated shade of blue. This creates a "blue" layer that is legible yet unobtrusive. Similarly, Point Reyes is labeled in green to associate it with the green park region, but more emphatically, as the destination for this map.

Get it right in black and white

The perceived lightness of a color is called *luminance or value*. Luminance can be measured, captured by technology such as black-and-white cameras, or computed. Reducing colors to their luminance values allows us to evaluate the contrast and spatial relationships in a design without the distraction of hue.

Consider the map in a luminance-only view, created by the Grayscale function in Adobe Photoshop. All the features are still legible and useful. The roads remain the dominant visual layer because they contrast strongly with the light gray land. The difference between Point Reyes and its surrounding ocean is more subtle than it is in color, but still distinct. It is now easy to see that the text labeling Point Reyes is darker (higher contrast) than the text labeling the Pacific Ocean, which gives it more emphasis.

Luminance contrast defines shape and edges, directing our attention and defining importance. Metrics for text legibility are defined with respect to luminance contrast. Adding color cannot repair a design that is poorly organized or lacks a clear information hierarchy. Designers in many fields call the need to focus on contrast rather than colors "get it right in black and white."

Do no harm

Edward Tufte, in his classic book *Envisioning Information*, begins his chapter on color with the admonition: "Above all, do no harm." Color used well can enhance and beautify, but color used poorly can be worse than no color at all.

Beautifully colored but unreadable information is of no use to anyone. You must take special care when coloring text to maintain sufficient luminance contrast for legibility. If text is displayed on a background that varies in lightness or color (like all too many PowerPoint templates suggest), its prominence and legibility will shift with its placement. When coloring individual words for emphasis, be sure they are still readable—and never randomly color individual words or letters unless you intend to be confusing.

If you **can't** use color wisely,
it is best to **avoid** it entirely
Above all, do **no** harm

If you can't use color wisely,
it is best to avoid it entirely
Above all, do no harm

If you can't use color wisely,
it is best to avoid it entirely
Above all, do no harm.

When using color as labels, apply it consistently and deliberately. Remember that text and symbols in the same or similar colors will appear related, so be sure they actually are. Define what each color represents and create a color palette for your design. Important information should be indicated by location, size, and contrast, not by applying bright colors.

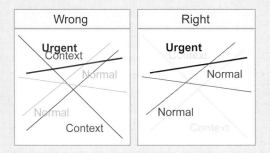

Wrong	Right
Urgent Context Normal Normal Context	**Urgent** Context Normal Normal Context

Color division deficiency

Between 8–10 percent of men and approximately 1 percent of women have some form of color vision deficiency (CVD) or colorblindness. Most have difficulty distinguishing red from green, and distinguishing those colors from orange-yellow. Dichromats see only two colors, most commonly blue and orange (plus gray). People with mild cases of CVD see strong colors but not pastels, and they have difficulty distinguishing colors that vary only by the addition of red or green, such as blue and purple, brown and gray, or the many shades of blue-green. People with CVD, however, have no trouble interpreting luminance—yet another reason to "get it right in black and white." Programs such as Vischeck (www.vischeck.com) simulate the common forms of CVD. For example, the following figure illustrates how a deuteranope would see the colored text to the left. Unless you know that all your viewers have normal color vision, be sure your message is intelligible to all.

If you **can't** use **color** wisely,
it is best to avoid it entirely
Above all, do **no** harm

In conclusion

Color is beautiful and digital media makes it easy to include it in all forms of presentations and designs. Skillful use of color, however, can only be achieved by combining principles with practice. Remember, most ideas can be well presented in black and white. Add color carefully and for a purpose, and your results will be both beautiful and functional.

Achieving an Emotional Connection

Color can be used to emphasize, get attention, point the way, and so on, but color is also emotional. We do not want to make too much of this, as it's impossible to list all the associations regarding color. These associations and feelings can be very culture specific and interpretations can vary somewhat depending on your particular audience. Still, here are a few generally accepted associations, both negative and positive. Proper usage depends on you researching your audience to find out if there are any colors to avoid, emphasize, and so on.

 Red: Assertive, powerful, bold, urgent, intense, emotionally hot, love, and passion—but also stop, danger, evil, murder, and so on. Depending on your message, an association with red such as "blood red" can be positive in a Red Cross blood drive presentation, or it might be negative in the case of war or death.

 Pink: Romantic, soft, tranquil, passive, femininity, health, love, romance, joy, and cotton candy.

 Orange: Warmth, compassion, excitement, enthusiasm, spiritual, energized, playful, fun, autumn, and Halloween. Orange is often used for sports teams, such as the OSU Beavers, the Syracuse Orangemen, the University of Tennessee Volunteers, and the Denver Broncos, because of its energy.

 Green: Natural, balance, harmony, the environment, earthy, healthy, persistent, calm, good luck, rebirth, go (as in traffic light), and spring—but also the color of envy.

 Blue: Dignified, professional, successful, loyal, calm, peaceful, tranquil, positive, and authoritative (in dark blue)—but also melancholy (as in feeling blue).

Yellow: Optimistic, cheerful, happy, energetic, fun, sunshine, inspiring, summer, and gold—but also cautious (used a lot on warning signs because yellow gets attention).

 Purple: Meditative, royalty, luxury, wisdom, spiritual, exotic, creativity, artistic, inspiration, and spirituality.

 Brown: Natural, earthy, solid, reliable, strong, comfortable, rustic—but also bland, conservative, and ordinary.

 Black: Classy, formal, artistic, simplicity, authority, and power—but also negatives such as death, fright, loss, troubles, and mourning.

White: Pure, innocent, clean, new, simple, spacious, cool, and winter (snow)—but also bland, ordinary, and sterile (good if you're a medical professional). In some cultures it is associated with death.

 Gray: Neutral, respect, humility, stable, wise, and simple—but also uncommitted, cloudy, dull, depression, or a general negative feeling of a "lack of color."

Image in slide from iStockphoto.com.

Feel warm and stay cool

It's useful to understand that colors can be broadly categorized in terms of their relative warmth and coolness. Colors closer to red, orange, yellow, and brown are warm, and colors closer to blue, green, and violet are cool. Warm colors tend to pop out a bit and come toward you. Cool colors tend to fade into the background. For this reason, cool colors are often used for backgrounds and warm colors are often used for foreground elements.

Artists use warm and cool colors to create depth and volume in paintings, and we can do the same by observing the relationship between warm and cool colors in a slide design. You can use warm colors for backgrounds as long as you adjust the value and saturation appropriately. As a general principle, however, remember that warmer colors come to the foreground, so it's usually a good idea to use those colors for emphasis.

Beyond this, people develop certain feelings about warm and cool colors. Many of our color impressions may be learned (for example, reading the previous information about the emotions tied to colors may influence the way you think about them). Nonetheless, people's feelings about and associations with color are genuine. For example, some people associate blues and greens with cool aspects found in nature such as grass, trees, and the clear blue sky. Warm colors of orange and yellow are associated with the heat of the sun. Red may be associated with hot things in nature such as lava, fire, and "red hot" chili peppers (the hottest ones are actually not red, but they'll turn your face quite red indeed). You can work those emotional aspects of color into your slide designs if they make sense and support your message.

In this slide, I took two scenes from nature—one blue and cool and one orange and warm—and layered them differently. You can see how cool colors fade to the background and warm colors pop, despite their placement on the slide.

Lights on or off?

If the projector is bright—or if you are using a large flat-panel display—there is little need to darken the room. Whenever possible, do not turn the lights off. Communication is enhanced when audiences can clearly see both the visuals and your face. (And it certainly makes for better teaching if students can see the teacher.)

Slide background color: light or dark?

For large keynote presentations at conferences, darker venues (Pecha Kucha Nights or Ignite events, for example), and larger venues, use a darker slide background because white light on the background can be blinding in an otherwise dark room. Most situations, however, such as those in college lecture halls or in school classrooms, have enough ambient light to justify a white or light background.

The advantage of using a white background is that you can use stock images without having to take time to remove the white backgrounds. (PowerPoint and Keynote come with tools for removing a selected color from an image, such as a white background, but their tools do not do as smooth a job as more professional editing software.) Regardless of the type of background you choose, what matters most is maintaining clear contrast between the background and the foreground elements. It's important to pay attention, then, to the levels of contrast among the foreground elements and the background.

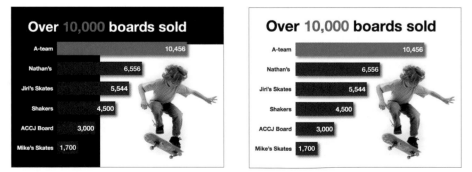

Images in slides on this page and opposite page from iStockphoto.com.

On a large screen, the chart in the slide on the left does work, though the contrast is more subtle for the gray bars. The background pattern in the slide on the right makes it harder to see the gray bars.

The slide on the left has a background with a midtone of gray, which makes the gray bars almost impossible to see. The background in the slide on the right contrasts well with the darker gray bars.

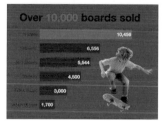

As I'm sure is obvious to you, the brightness of the backgrounds in these slides is neither attractive nor easy to view for extended periods when placed behind this particular chart.

The color of the text in the slide on the left matches the color of the hills in the distance. The text is legible, but pops out much better in white, as seen on the right.

A shadow is added to the text on the left to make it pop out more and add depth. Greater contrast is created by placing the text in a box with a darker background on the right.

Working with Color

Slideware comes with a wide range of templates and preselected color palettes, and you can make your own simple color palettes as well. An easy but underutilized technique is to create a unique color palette from a few colors in one of your photographs. Choose colors that you think set the appropriate tone for the visual presentation. To do this, click the color picker or eye dropper on the desired portions of the image. If, for example, you are not required to use a company template but still prefer to use a color palette that works well with the colors of the company logo or other elements of brand identity, you can easily extract the colors from the logo and add them to your presentation's palette.

Pick colors using your images

Let's say I am giving a presentation on the benefits of eating a traditional Japanese diet. I might start with a photo of salmon since it has the same look and feel as other images I'll be using in the talk. To create a suitable palette, I can click on the salmon, the greens, the lemon, and more neutral areas of the image such as the bowl, plate, or table.

Using colors taken from the actual photograph of the salmon (plus white), I created a simple color scheme that is in harmony with other similar images used in the presentation. (Images in slides from iStockphoto.com.)

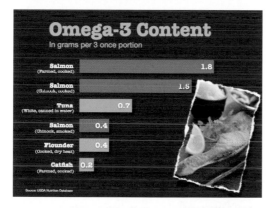

Create themes with cool online resources

You can find terrific books on color theory, written for both trained designers and people with little or no experience. Let's face it: Most working professionals do not have the time to delve deeply into a study of the complexities of using color. The good news is you can use online resources to create harmonious color themes without having advanced knowledge in color theory.

There are a few really good online resources such as ColorSchemer (www.colorschemer.com) and COLOURlovers (colourlovers.com), but my personal favorite is Kuler (http://kuler.adobe.com). Kuler is a Web-based color tool from Adobe that has thousands of community-generated color themes that you can search. The best thing about Kuler is that you can easily make your own themes. Once you register with Kuler, you can begin to create your own color themes or palettes, and store, view, and retrieve all your saved themes in your personal *Mykuler* space.

You can also use Kuler to create a color palette from colors in an image that is key to your presentation. While you can do this in slideware, Kuler offers additional features and the ability to tweak the colors. Here are the basic steps:

1. Click Create. On the next screen, click From an Image. You can either click Upload or Flickr to upload your photograph.

2. Kuler automatically extracts colors and generates a theme of five colors from the image.

3. Adjust the theme (if you want) by changing what Kuler calls the "mood." You can select from Colorful, Bright, Muted, Deep, and Dark moods, which are based on the colors extracted from your image.

4. Save the theme to your account. You can share it with the community if you like, and even download it as an Adobe Swatch Exchange file as well.

5. To get the theme into your slideware, write down the color values from Kuler (you'll find the values when you click the little slider icon in Kuler) and then create those colors in your program's color palette (entering the values into your RGB sliders). You can also simply take a screenshot of the theme and then use your slideware's color picker to save the colors into a new theme for your presentation.

Creating themes with Kuler

The Kuler Web site allows you to select a color and then apply harmony rules such as Analogous, Monochromatic, Triad, Complementary, Compound, and Shades that are based on some of the basic, tried-and-true principles of color theory discussed earlier. All you have to do, then, is select a base color and a color rule to quickly create harmonious themes.

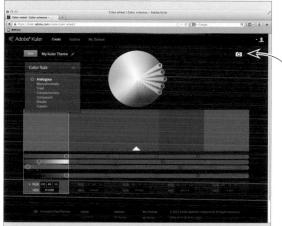

Click here to create colors from a photo.

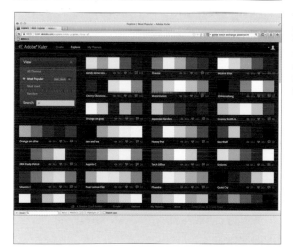

You can experiment and make your own combinations and themes or you can browse the many themes generated by the community. You can search by most popular (pictured here) or most used, most recent, etc.

Here, I selected a photo that I snapped at the beach in Oregon. I liked the natural tones of the sand and the water and the bit of fog that was rolling in. The red/orange from the rescue vehicle provides a good accent color. From the Color Mood menu on the left I chose Dark.

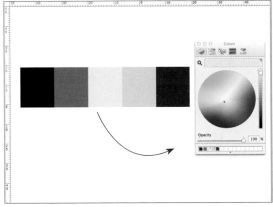

I simply took a screen capture of the color theme, placed it into the slideware (Keynote in this case) and used the color picker to save each of the five colors one-by-one to use anytime I need.

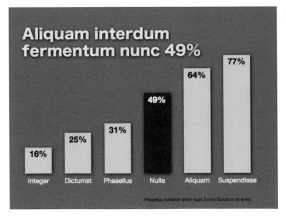

A sample slide using the theme from above.

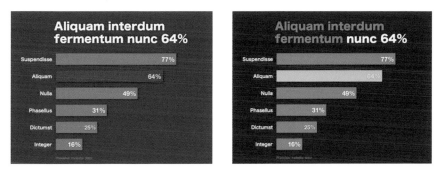

This slide uses three colors from a theme called "Organic" plus white. I'm not crazy about it, but it could be used in a presentation on something like organic farming.

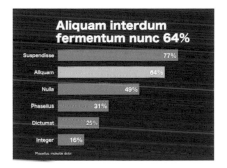
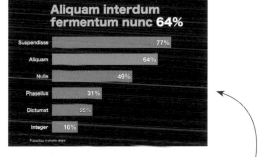

The sample slides above use colors from two themes I created in Kuler from a photo of Haystack Rock (right), plus white for the labels. More black was added to the background color in the second slide to increase the contrast with the foreground.

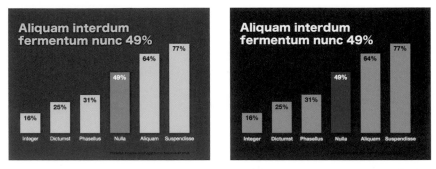

The colors in the slide on the left were taken from a popular Kuler theme called "Zen Garden." For the slide on the right, the colors were picked from the Kuler theme "Cherry Cheese Cake."

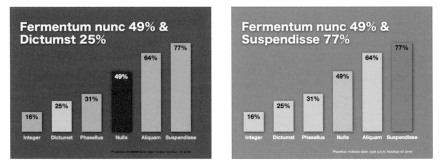

The colors in the slide on the left were taken from the Kuler theme called "Tech Office." And the colors in the slide on the right were picked from the theme "Watermelon."

Experiment and play with the tools

You can spend hours playing around with Kuler. This is not wasted time if it helps you see how adjusting hue, value, and saturation creates color harmonies. For actual presentation themes, keep the number of different hues to a minimum. The mantra is to always use color for a reason and with restraint. To teach yourself more about how colors can work together, however, it's OK to go a little wild sometimes while you're experimenting. Kuler has a great community and it's a wonderful online tool from which to learn.

In Sum

- Follow the tenets of the Zen aesthetic, including simplicity and the idea of maximum effect with minimum means. Powerful visual messages can be created with a single "color" in the form of different shades and tints. It is the value contrast that really distinguishes the foreground from the background.

- You can create harmonious relationships with color combinations such as monochromatic and analogous. The way you use color helps to unify your presentations, emphasize important points, and balance the elements.

- You can achieve an emotional connection with your audience by using specific colors or by focusing on a warm or cool theme. Warm colors tend to pop out a bit and come toward you; cool colors tend to fade into the background. For this reason, cool colors are often chosen for backgrounds and warm colors are often used for foreground elements.

- Great resources exist for creating harmonious color themes without requiring much knowledge of color theory. You can create themes with your own photos or videos directly in your slideware, or use one of the many online tools available such as Kuler.

4

Using Images to Tell Stories

When I was 17, I created my first multimedia presentation. It consisted of slides for a big project for my high school biology class. The presentation was on issues related to the effects of pollution on the environment. The slide show was a visual affirmation of all the natural beauty around us juxtaposed with the needless manmade destruction to showcase the hypocrisy of human actions.

I created this presentation before the dawn of the digital age, when personal computers were not yet used in schools. So, when I say slides I mean real slides: 35mm transparencies that loaded into a round slide projector called a carousel. The presentation used two carousels working in sync to achieve the effect of a smooth cross-dissolve transition between slides. I added a prerecorded sound track and synchronized the music and images with the transitions on a single screen. It was simple, beautifully visual, and highly effective. The resolution of the photographic images was fantastic. It looked nearly as good as anything created today—but it was a ton of work and the presentation could not really be shared unless I lugged around a bunch of equipment with my teacher's help.

This was about eight years before Microsoft released PowerPoint, so I had no examples of how to create and deliver a multimedia presentation. Instead, I tried to glean visual storytelling and reporting techniques from network news programs and documentary films. The idea of using bullet points and long lines of text never occurred to me. The slides, after all, were to be a visual complement to the narrative. The slides were meant to illustrate, show evidence, and evoke emotions. I told the story.

Instead of titles and bullet points, my instructor talked about research, evidence, structure, and story—about having a point that moves people from point A to point B. The photographic slides produced by my 35mm camera were the only visuals I was allowed to use for the assignment.

Because film was expensive—and I had to wait two weeks for the slides to return from the lab—I thought carefully about the story I wanted to tell and the types of images I needed to support my argument, make my case, and tell my story. Only after I did my research and completed the plan on paper, did I set out with my camera to find evidence of the problem, taking pictures of what society had to lose (the beauty) and evidence of the threats to it (the pollution).

Long before I ever heard of concepts such as the cognitive load theory or the dual channels of cognition, like most students, I knew intuitively and through experience that quality images plus narration was better than narration plus a lot of text onscreen, even though I was years away from experiencing "death by PowerPoint."

These slides are from an updated version of that first multimedia presentation I did back in high school. I used the lyrics from a Tower of Power song called "Can't Stand to See the Slaughter" to introduce the theme of the talk. (Images in slides from iStockphoto.com.)

The Visual Matters

Traditional literacy is important, of course, but today multimedia literacy—text, audio, and images, including video—is just as important for learning, teaching, and communicating both complex and simple ideas. Some might consider it even more important. Multimedia is immediate and rich, and it enables us to amplify and clarify the meaning of content in ways text or narration alone cannot. The language of the 21st century includes images like never before. The legendary Will Eisner writes in his book *Graphic Storytelling and Visual Narrative* (W.W. Norton & Co., 2008): "The proliferation of the use of images as a communicant was propelled by the growth of technology that required less in text-reading skills...visual literacy has entered the panoply of skills required for communication in this century."

High-quality images make it possible for us to become true digital storytellers. The late Dana Atchley, the father of the digital storytelling movement, coined the term *digital storytelling* and according to him, "...digital storytelling combines the best of two worlds: the 'new world' of digitized video, photography, and art, and the 'old world' of telling stories. This means the 'old world' of PowerPoint slides filled with bullet point statements will be replaced by a new world of examples via stories, accompanied by evocative images and sounds."

Atchley was right. While there are still too many uninspiring presentations that use a strict bulleted format or are overly cluttered, more and more people are getting the message about the need to become better storytellers. They are starting to understand the profound power the effective use of multimedia has for helping us tell better stories.

Storytelling is a shared experience between speaker and listener. Images can help make that experience more powerful because they help us connect better with our audience. In the book *Going Visual* (Wiley, 2005), authors Alexis Gerard and Bob Goldstein have this to say about using images:

> ...images have a unique power not just to convey information, but also to build unity and consensus around that information to promote action and decision making.... Because images are complete and detailed and deliver an information experience that has greater impact than words, a common base of visual information proves to be the most efficient form of shared experience from which to make decisions.

Gerard and Goldstein explain that the evolution of visual communication technology consists of three main elements:

- Skill level—technology has made visual communication easier to produce.
- Time requirements—creating and using images takes less time today.
- Audience reach—technology now allows us to communicate with more people visually.

In one of my past presentations I showed the evolution of visual communication as explained in *Going Visual.* To do this, I created these simple slides that were very effective at instantly showing that we have indeed come a long way in the evolution of visual communication.

Slides adapted from *Going Visual* by Gerard and Goldstein. (Images in slides from iStockphoto.com.)

We Are Visual Beings

Vision is our most powerful sense. Therefore, designing messages that include images is a highly effective way to get people's attention and help them understand and remember your content. Most live slideware presentations today still contain a lot of text. However, according to Dr. John Medina, author of the best-selling *Brain Rules: 12 Principles for Surviving and Thriving at Work, Home, and School* (Pear Press, 2008), this is inefficient because our brains are not as good at identifying letters and words as identifying and remembering pictures. Says Medina, "Professionals everywhere need to know about the incredible inefficiency of text-based information and the incredible effects of images." Dr. Medina says that all professionals should "burn their current PowerPoint presentations" and instead create slides that take advantage of our incredible ability to understand images. Each presentation case is different; however, evidence shows that we should strongly consider the use of images in the design of presentation visuals.

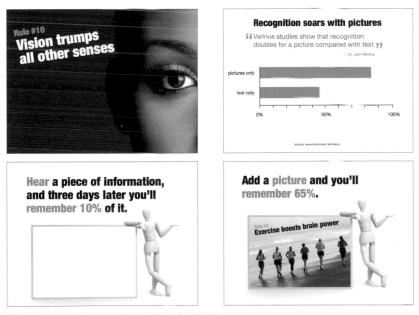

Slides adapted from *Brain Rules* by Dr. John Medina.
(Images in slides from iStockphoto.com.)

Power of the Photograph

I love still images because the photograph captures a moment in time, allowing the viewer to slow down and think and wonder and reflect. Many filmmakers—especially documentary filmmakers—use still photos as a complement to motion pictures or video. Photos allow for greater emphasis and may have less distracting elements, giving the presenter or narrator/filmmaker more freedom to augment the photo for a desired effect. Still images also allow the viewer time to interpret their own meaning from the image. We can learn a lot from documentary film, especially from the kind created by Ken Burns, whose films rely heavily on still images.

One tip is to avoid the usage of imagery only as ornamentation. What you see in a Ken Burns film is a simple and powerful use of photos and other imagery that support the narrative and illuminate the story on a visceral level, thereby making the experience richer and more memorable. When we hear a story that is amplified by compelling photography, the issue in the story becomes less of an abstraction. The issue becomes more concrete and emotional. The next time you give a presentation about an important but complex topic—especially a social issue—see if you can illuminate the general topic by focusing on a particular story. This is a technique that storytellers, such as filmmakers, often use. Powerful images plus thoughtful narration—and maybe even a bit of text—can help you tell your story in ways that bullet points never can.

The use of large images in these slides make an especially powerful impact.
(Images in slides from iStockphoto.com.)

Full-bleed images offer ultimate impact

Margins around an image give it a sort of protective frame. When you compare two or more images on slides, margins are necessary to clearly differentiate among the images. Generally, however, people use images that are too small, making it hard for audiences to see the content, thereby reducing the impact of the photo.

When it makes sense to do so, I suggest you *bleed* images off the edge of the slide frame. That is, fill the entire slide area with the image. (Bleed is actually a term that comes from the printing world. In a book like this one, when you want to fill an entire page with an image, you must use an image that is just a tiny bit larger than the area of the page. In other words, you bleed the image off the page to make sure none of the underlying paper color shows through the trimmed page, which would destroy the effect.) With slides, all you need is an image that is exactly the same size as the slide. If your slides are 1024 x 768 pixels, for example, then the dimensions of the image need to be at least this large to fill the screen. A full-bleed or full-screen image gives the illusion that the slide is bigger than it is. This is especially true if part of the subject in your image runs off the screen. For example, a burger shop may make a poster featuring a picture of their "Enormo Burger," but with part of the burger bleeding off the edge to suggest that it's so big it can't fit within the frame. This makes the image more compelling and it draws the viewer in.

The image in this slide bleeds off the edges, making the slide feel bigger. (Image in slides from iStockphoto.com.)

Here is an example of a smaller image producing less impact. Which slide better reflects the idea of an enormous burger?

Here, the image is framed against the background slide template. The background is a distraction.

Using a white background creates more of a formal border, which emphasizes the photo.

This is a partial bleed. The photo makes a bigger impression, yet still has a border at the bottom.

I prefer a white partial border as it seems more harmonious with this image and more professional.

With a full-bleed (or full-screen) image, the background slide is gone. Now the image becomes the background and the type becomes part of the image, creating a more dynamic, engaging visual that is easily seen from the back of the room.

Here, the image is rather small and the background template from the slideware is "noisy" due to all the gridlines.

The image is at least larger, as is the text, but it is still not a very clean slide.

This is not bad. The template is gone and the image has a frame, which makes it seem like a snapshot from the station. The text is easy to see.

Here, the image is even larger, filling the whole screen from left to right, and the text looks good. The highlight color (green) is taken from the train.

Now the image takes up the entire screen for a more dynamic effect. The type is easy to see in both cases, but a black box is added to the version on the right for even better legibility.

This is an example of taking a busy slide and breaking it up over several slides (in this case, four slides). The slide on the left repeats many of the things the presenter will share with the audience before he describes the efficient rail system that moves an incredible amount of people all around the city each day. But instead of using loads of text on a slide, he uses large dynamic visuals in harmony with the flow of his narrative. There are now four slides. First he explains what is meant by "Greater Tokyo." Then he takes the audience onto the train platform to give them a feel for the crowds. The slide than fades to a blurry version of the same photo so that the text—his key point— can be seen easily. The last side appears as he emphasizes just how large a number 40 million is by comparing it to the population of New Zealand.

AFTER ▾

(Images in slides from iStockphoto.com.)

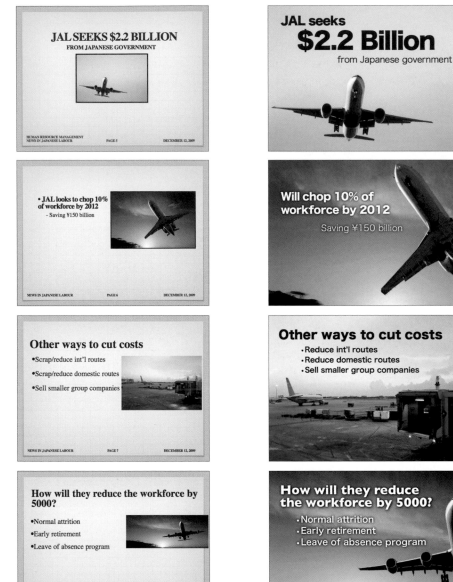

The slides in the left column are the originals. Note how the message in each slide has greater impact when the image fills the slide (right column). (Images in slides from iStockphoto.com.)

The ideal resolution for projection

As a general rule, use images that are 72 ppi to 100 ppi with dimensions that are the same or very close to the slide dimensions. For example, 800 x 600 or 1024 x 768 when you want to use an image that fills your entire slide (a slide with an aspect ratio of 4:3). For slides with a more cinematic aspect ratio of 16:9—an aspect ratio increasingly common at large events such as TED or professional conferences—photos may need to be at least 1280 x 720, a popular resolution for a 16:9 screen.

Flickr offers millions of searchable images with a Creative Commons license. When you find an image you like, right-click (Control-click) the image to see all the sizes available for that image. In the example on the left (one of my snaps from Sydney), the largest size in this case is 1200 x 768. My slide dimensions are 1024 x 768, so this image will work fine. Once in slideware (below left) you can see that the image is a bit wider than the slide, but I can simply move the image to the left to get the framing I want. Simple.

Improve images through cropping

Cropping is a technique for reframing or adjusting the composition of an original photograph. Of course, it's always better to take the perfect shot or purchase the perfect image, but that does not always happen. Cropping changes the image to better suit your needs. For example, you may have images of interesting subjects, but the composition is not what you had hoped. I have loads of holiday snapshots that are not that great, but can be improved with a bit of cropping.

I took this shot of Bondi Beach in Australia a few years ago using a simple digital point-and-shoot camera. The original resolution was 300 ppi, measuring 2816 x 2112 pixels. The size of the file was 4.2 MB. For images that will be placed in slideware, a resolution of 72 ppi or 96 ppi is usually fine. So I first reduced the resolution to 72 ppi, which decreased the file size to 1.9 MB. Next, I decreased the dimensions of the slide to something closer to 1024 x 768, the size of my slides, using basic photo-editing software. Because I started with such a large image, however, I can go inside the photograph and frame it in a way that is a little more interesting and specific. Using the cropping tool, I selected an area of the photograph that shows only the surfer, leaving plenty of empty space in case I want to place text inside the image. Now, the image measures just a bit over 1024 x 768 and the JPEG file size is about 300 KB. I could reduce the file size further through more compression, but this would decrease the quality of the image.

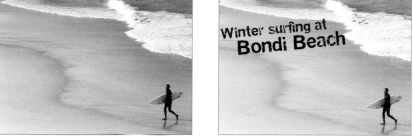

The large image is the original snap I took at the beach. The image below is the cropped version of the image, which is now the same size as the slide on the right (1024 x 768 at 72 ppi).

Basic image file types

Of the many different image file formats, you really only need to be familiar with a few:

- **JPEG.** The most common image file format you will work with is JPEG (.jpg). JPEG stands for Joint Photographic Experts Group, but you do not need to remember that part. Just remember that JPEGs (jay-pegs) use "lossy" compression, which means that a bit of image quality is lost during compression. Usually, the loss in picture quality is only noticeable when you are using a high level of compression. JPEG is the preferred format for photographs used on Web pages. Small JPEGs may look great on a Web site, but they usually look horrible if you significantly increase the image size for a slide. When you're selecting large images for slides, make sure the size and resolution of the original image will work. JPEG compression does a good job with photographs, especially when you have lots of colors blending into each other, soft shadows, and so on.

- **PNG.** PNG, which stands for Portable Network Graphics, features lossless compression. While I most often use JPEGs for onscreen presentations in slideware, I do occasionally use the PNG (.png) format to achieve a transparency effect, such as those shown below.

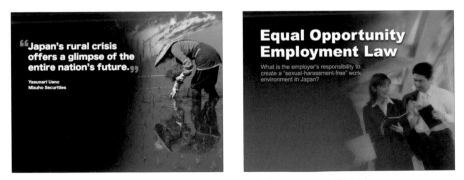

The images in these slides are PNG files. I created the gradient transparency effect in Photoshop. The PNG and TIFF formats support these kinds of transparency effects. (Images in slides from iStockphoto.com.)

- **TIFF.** If you need to print images, I recommend the TIFF format (.tif), which stands for Tagged Image File Format. Use TIFF files for printing images in CMYK. (TIFF files can include an alpha channel for transparency effects and can work in slideware, but the TIFF files are much larger than PNG files.) TIFF files can be compressed without losing picture quality; however, compared to JPEGs, TIFF files can be much larger. Larger file sizes will not usually create problems, especially with newer computers, but there is no reason to create unnecessarily large files. On older computers, larger image files can slow things down a bit.

- **GIF.** GIF, which stands for Graphics Interchange Format, is a file format used mainly for the Web. The GIF format may be appropriate for line art with very sharp edges and large areas of the same color. GIF reduces the colors in an image down to 256, so it is not good for photographs.

- **EPS.** EPS stands for Encapsulated PostScript. You may run into the EPS format when you purchase line art or vector graphics or create your own line drawings in an application such as Adobe Illustrator. An EPS file can hold photographic information as well, but you are most likely to see this format used for vector graphics. The advantage of vector graphics is that you can greatly increase the image scale without decreasing the image quality. To illustrate this, I took a vector graphic from iStockphoto and converted a copy of it to a small bitmap (JPEG) image. When I scale up the bitmap image, you see the quality is reduced as the pixels get larger. The vector image, however, looks great scaled because it uses mathematical formulas to make sure all the points on the paths maintain their original relationships. The EPS format is good for drawings, but for photographs you'll stick primarily with good-quality JPEG files.

In this slide, the image on the left is a small JPEG that I stretched, resulting in some horrible pixelation. The vector version of the image on the right stays crisp at any size.

John McWade

Designer, author, world's first desktop publisher

www.bamagazine.com

John McWade is the founder and creative director of Before & After *magazine and the author of numerous books on graphic design. His latest book is* Before & After: How to Design Cool Stuff *(Peachpit Press, 2010).*

Picture your presentation

Better than charts and bullet points, photographs give your audience an emotional connection to your words. As presenters, we *love* data! Fifty-two base hits, 23 abandoned children, Class 3 hurricanes. We track data, we analyze it, we graph it—and we cheerfully present it to snoozing audiences everywhere. What's funny is that data alone has no value. Only in the context of real life does it have meaning. And real life is conveyed best not with data but with *story*.

To tell a story, you need the help of photos. Photos communicate on many channels. They wordlessly *draw the audience into your world,* make emotional connections, and prepare your listeners for what you have to say.

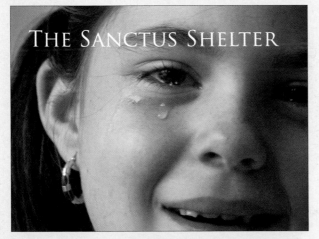

It's easy to find generically happy images, but the unseen sadness that everyone bears will rattle each audience member's soul. When pitching a program like the proposed shelter above, think first not in terms of dollars or "social units" or other statistical data but about who you're helping and why—then find an image to express it.

The top slide consists of only a fancy list of notes. The bottom slide with the orange inside the apple is surprising and familiar at the same time. The simple question—not a statement—gets the audience thinking and ready for what you'll say next.

You are the show

The first thing to understand is that you are the show; your audience has come to hear you, not read slides. Use a slide to fill the listener's mind with an image, then fill in the details orally. It's fun!

BEFORE ▾

This slide, which is basically the presentation notes, is visually useless. The information is fine, but it should come from you, where it can be accompanied by your personality, body language, and nuance. The correct use of a slide is to make a visual statement that words alone can't make.

AFTER ▾

We acquire Trax in 2010

Use a metaphorical image. Many topics don't have literal imagery that can be photographed. In these cases, you might try using visual metaphors. Think of your talk as having chapters, and use an image to introduce each one. The image provides a visual "hook" for the audience, who will relate everything you say back to the image.

Although it has no photo, this is a good slide because the chart is simple and clearly shows a trend. But oy vey! It's been a terrible year! It started bad and got worse, and, well, it's now so bad that the only thing to do is laugh...

...which is what a carefully selected image will have your audience doing. They'll remember this picture long after they've forgotten your charts, and because it's funny, you'll have their sympathy if not their help in solving your problems.

One thought at a time

Make one point per slide, even if you have room for more. This gives the viewer room to think and to "own" what you're saying, which are keys to good communication.

BEFORE ▼

Traffic Management Systems

Transportation	Passengers per week
Airplanes	589,000
Trains	377,800
Buses	320,900
Taxis	218,600

Planes, trains, buses, taxis, 589,000; 377,800; 320,900; 218,600—quick! got all that? It's useful information, but who will be moved by it, much less remember it? Put the data on four slides, one topic per slide, each accompanied by a descriptive, full-screen photo. This gives your viewer room to think and to own what you're saying.

AFTER ▼

Search using iStockphoto's CopySpace™

How does one find good photos? The artistic part is up to you, but iStockphoto's Search with CopySpace function can help with composition. Enter a keyword, specify what part of the photo you want to leave space for words, and click.

First, create a free account to use iStockphoto, then:

1. Click Advanced Search.

2. In Search with CopySpace, click grid squares to specify areas of the photo to remain blank (clicked squares turn green).

3. Enter a keyword such as "face" and watch what happens.

It's cool.

Common Image Mistakes

With the ubiquity of digital cameras and smartphones, and the plethora of photo Web sites, more people than ever are using images in presentations. That's good, but unfortunately, people often make the same mistakes with their images when using them in a slide presentation. We'll look at a few here.

Top things to avoid when using images

Let's imagine you are preparing a presentation for a large audience on current issues in Japanese education. One issue facing schools and universities in Japan today is the decreasing number of potential students. The source of the problem is low fertility rates, resulting in fewer children being born. So our sample slide touches on the low fertility rate in Japan in this context. For an effective slide, you could use either a full-bleed image like the one below of the two elementary students walking, or a smaller photograph of a school yard in Japan. We'll use the photo of the two kids walking to school as a starting point and then discuss the ten common mistakes to avoid.

Either of these two slides could work. Notice how the use of the images in these slides sharply contrasts with their use in the examples that follow. (Images in slides from iStockphoto.com.)

1. Image dimensions are too small

You do not have to do a full bleed with an image, but this particular image does not work at such a small size. (The slide is 800 x 600 while this image is 373 x 176.)

2. Image is placed randomly on the slide

The image is large enough to be seen easily, but it's placed willy-nilly on the slide. Usually, this causes the text to be lost in the background (although in this case the text is still legible) and the image placement appears accidental.

3. Image is almost full screen—but not quite

Nothing should look accidental. This looks like the presenter was going for a full bleed but just missed. Now, the slide's background template can be seen just enough to become a bit of noise. Make sure that your full-bleed images are indeed full bleed (that is, they fill 100 percent of the screen).

4. Image is pixelated due to low resolution

This happens when you take a low-resolution image (such as a JPEG from a Web site) and stretch it out. Oh, the humanity! Make sure you use an image that is large enough for your purposes.

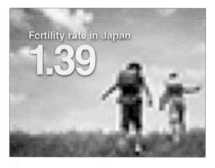

5. Using several small images in one slide

It's better for your audience if you use *one* (or perhaps two) large images rather than several small images. In most cases you get more impact and clarity from one clear, large image. (On your computer screen the images may look big enough, but that's because your nose is about 18 inches from the screen.) Using several images may introduce noise as well.

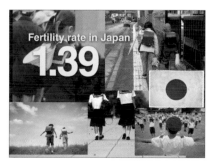

6. Image is pixelated and has a watermark

Even worse than using a pixelated image is taking a free preview from a photo Web site and stretching it out. This introduces distracting visual noise and communicates that you are cheap, lazy, or both. If you cannot afford images or do not have a camera or other image source, then it's better to use no images at all.

7. Image is distorted

Horizontal or vertical image stretching is all too common. This distortion occurs when people stretch an image to make it fit the dimensions of a slide without making sure the proportions stays constant. The image becomes a distraction and looks odd. (Are young Japanese students really 8 feet tall, or so wide?)

8. Use of the tile feature

Just because the software lets you tile an image, does not mean you should. Now the background image has too much going on (even if it did not have watermarks).

9. Use of clip art

Avoid off-the-shelf clip art. Your own sketches and drawings can be a refreshing change if used consistently throughout the visuals, but generic clip art is so last century.

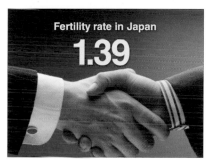

10. Image is a cliché or unrelated to the content

What do two businessmen shaking hands have to do with the fertility rate in Japan? Nothing. Yet even if the presentation is about a business partnership, the image is still a cliché.

11. The background image has too much going on and the text is hard to see

Sometimes, the image is actually pretty good, but it needs a little work to get the text to pop out more. The slide below on the left is not horrible, but the balance is off and the text is a little difficult to read. For the slide on the right, the image is cropped for better balance, giving more space for the text to breathe. In addition, the text is now in a transparent box so it pops out a bit more.

You don't take a photograph,
you make it.

— Ansel Adams

Making Your Own Images

You can purchase images or obtain them legally from various sources, but it's likely that you have your own camera as well. If you're working on a professional-level presentation, you may want to purchase good shots or hire a photographer. In many cases, however, you will be able to use your own photographs.

You may not be the world's greatest photographer, but that's OK. You can learn to get better. One of the keys to good shots—like design itself—is to keep things simple. Scott Kelby is a leading authority on digital photography and he says that clutter and distraction are the things that most often kill properly exposed shots.

> Look for simplicity in your backgrounds, in your people shots, in your architectural elements, in every aspect—the simpler the surroundings, the more powerful the impact.... Look for the absence of distraction. Look for the absence of clutter and noise, watch for distracting elements that sneak into the top and sides of your frame, and create some photos that have great impact—not because of what they have, but because of what they don't have—lots of junk.
>
> — Scott Kelby

On the next four pages, photographer Scott Kelby offers valuable tips for taking better photos.

Scott Kelby

Photographer and editor-in-chief of both *Photoshop User* and *Layers* magazines, and president of the National Association of Photoshop Professionals (NAPP)

www.scottkelby.com

Scott Kelby is the world's No. 1 best-selling author of computer and technology books, and is the author of the all-time best-selling book on digital photography: The Digital Photography Book, Volume 1 *(Peachpit Press, 2006). Here Scott gives simple tips for taking better photos.*

10 tricks for getting better-looking photos

A lot of people have been going through a very frustrating experience with their digital cameras. They started with a small 3 or 4 megapixel point-and-shoot compact camera, and they were disappointed with the images they were getting. So they went out and bought a newer point-and-shoot, or a more expensive Digital SLR camera (with interchangeable lenses) that's 10 or 12 megapixels and now they're disappointed with their larger-size images. The problem is, it's not about the camera. They both take pictures of whatever you aim them at.

However, the fact that it's "not about the camera" is good news for all of us, because that means that no matter which camera you own, you can learn to take better-looking photos now, today—and here. I've included some of my favorite tips for doing just that.

1. Getting better portraits outside

Direct sunlight creates really harsh shadows— it's about the most unflattering light you can shoot someone in (only photograph people you don't like in direct sunlight). So, how do you get around this? Have your subject step into the shade. Under a tree, under an overhang, or any place where they're in complete shade (with no dapples of light coming through the branches of the tree). The difference is pretty staggering.

In the example you see below, on the left our subject is standing in direct sunlight. On the right, I had her move under a tree about 30 feet away. That's the only thing that I did differently, and look at the results.

2. Where to put your subject in the photo

When we first started taking photos of people, at some point somebody told us to make sure that our subject is in the center of the photo. That's how your average person takes a "people photo," which is one reason why these photos look so average. If you look at photos taken by professional photographers, you'll notice they usually place the person on the left or right side of the photo, rather than in the center. This adds interest and energy to the photo, and focuses your attention right on the subject (try this next time you're shooting a portrait—you'll be amazed at what a difference this one little thing makes).

3. The secret to shooting in low light

If you're shooting in a church, or at night, or even at dawn or dusk, you're going to get blurry photos. That's because the shutter needs to stay open longer to let more light in, and even the tiniest little movement on your part guarantees a blurry photo. The way around this is to put your camera on a tripod, which simply holds your camera steady. You don't have to buy an expensive one; my most famous photo was taken with a $14 tripod I bought at Walmart when I forget my regular tripod while on vacation.

4. The trick to getting great color

If you look at your photos, and they all look too blue, or too green, or too yellow, you're not alone. It's a common problem with digital cameras, but it's so easy to fix. All you have to do is change your camera's White Balance setting for the light you're shooting in. For example, if you're shooting in the shade, everything's going to have a blue tint to it. But if you

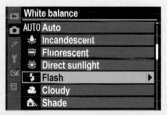

change the White Balance setting to Shade it changes the color so it looks great. If you're shooting indoors, change it to the Indoor setting (usually an icon of a light bulb). Shooting in an office? To keep everybody from looking green, change the White Balance to Fluorescent. If you're outside, you can just leave it set to Auto. Make setting the White Balance a part of your shooting routine, and your color will finally look great, no matter where you're shooting.

5. Better shots with your pop-up flash

That flash on top of your camera is really harsh. In fact, it may be the only light more harsh than direct sunlight, but there is something you can do to make it much more flattering. A company called LumiQuest (www.lumiquest.com) makes a small diffuser called a Soft Screen that fits over your camera's pop-up flash to soften and diffuse the light. The results you get are dramatically better—and your pictures are much more flattering to the subjects.

6. Don't make this mistake when shooting portraits

One of the biggest mistakes people make when taking portraits is that they leave too much room above the subject's head. Ideally, your subject's eyes would be in the top third of the photo, and your subject would pretty much fill the frame. Also, it's OK to crop off the top of your subject's head a bit (just look at the ads in any magazine),

but never chop off his or her chin. Also, the most important thing to have in focus is your subject's eyes, so make sure your focus point is on the eyes (this goes for shooting wildlife, too).

7. Golden rule of landscape photography

If you want much better landscape photos, the trick is to shoot your landscape in beautiful light, and that light happens twice a day: around sunrise and sunset. These are the only two times professional landscape photographers will even take landscape photos—that's how big a difference it makes (and that's why the pros call these two times of day "The Golden Hours"). Also, these are two times of day when the light will be lower, so you'll also need to shoot these shots on a tripod to keep from having blurry photos. Do these two things, and you'll be amazed at the difference in your photos (and so will your friends).

8. Use your camera's presets

If you want average-looking photos, leave your camera set to what your average camera owner does: Auto mode. But, if you want to take the quality of your images up a big notch, just turn the dial on the top of your camera to match

what you're shooting. When you do this, it changes your camera to the optimum settings for what you're shooting. If you're shooting people, switch that dial on top to the little icon of a person. Simple. If you're shooting a landscape, switch it to landscape (the icon usually looks like mountains). For shooting something really close up (like a flower), switch it to the flower icon. You'll be surprised at what a difference this makes, yet most people never spend the two seconds it takes to make this simple change.

9. Where to put the horizon line

When shooting a landscape, your average person puts the horizon line right in the center of the photo, right? Right. But if you don't want an average-looking photo, put your horizon line either at the top third of your photo or the bottom third. How do you know which one to use? If the sky is interesting with lots of clouds, put the horizon line at the bottom, so you see more sky. If you've got a boring, cloudless sky, put the horizon line at the top third, so you see more foreground instead. It's as simple as that. Just remember; there's a reason they call it "dead" center.

10. Change your vantage point

One thing that makes photos look average is that we all pretty much take our photos from the same view—standing. If we walk up on a flower, we shoot down at it from a standing position. If we're shooting a photo of our children, we stand there and shoot down on them. That's how we regularly see them, so the photos look regular. A great trick to make your photos more interesting is to simply change your angle to one that isn't so average. Get down on one knee to shoot your children at their eye view. Shoot flowers down low—at their level, so you show a view most folks don't see. Shoot down from a stairway on a street scene. This simple change of perspective gives a fresh, more professional look to your images.

To create a more interesting composition, put your horizon line either at the top third of your photo or the bottom third.

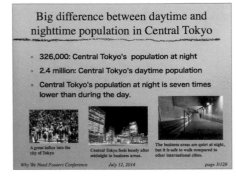

Here is another example of taking one busy slide with small, hard-to-see images and breaking it up into several slides. The examples below serve as a dynamic backdrop for the presenter as he discusses the great shift of people in and out of Tokyo. In this case, the presenter uses four slides, which he advances smoothly with his narrative, to create a more dynamic and even cinematic effect.

AFTER ▾

(Images in slides from iStockphoto.com.)

In Sum

- Avoid using imagery only as ornamentation. When we hear a story amplified by compelling photography, the issue becomes less of an abstraction and more concrete. It is emotional and it is memorable. Try to illuminate the general by focusing on the particular in your choice of imagery.

- Use full-bleed (full-screen) images for greater impact and try cropping images to create more compelling photographs.

- Don't be afraid to take your own photographs and use them in your presentations. Keep in mind that one of the keys to taking great shots is to "keep it simple," a lesson you can apply to many aspects of design.

- Try taking one busy slide and breaking the information up over several slides to match your narrative flow.

5

Making an Impact with Video

The power of the motion picture—or video—is undeniable. In a 2011 short video presented by Cisco called "The Power of Video," theoretical physicist Michio Kaku urges us to use video and other images in our communications. "The Power of video is the power of the mind itself," says Dr. Kaku. "A huge chunk of the brain power we have sitting on our shoulders is devoted to processing visual images. It's how we communicate. It's how we share information. It defines who we are." Dr. Kaku suggests that even the most complicated theories can be expressed simply through visualizations of some kind, including video. "All the great theories of the world are not equations," says Dr. Kaku, "[rather] they are based on simple principles which can be manifested as pictures, as video images...it's by images—pictures, video—that we understand the universe."

Video is ubiquitous in our professional and personal lives but it's still underutilized in presentations today. At least good use of video is underutilized. Many people, including teachers and especially students, use video effectively, but, for too many people, the idea of using video in a presentation seems too cumbersome to even bother spending much time with it. In this chapter we will look at why, when, and how to use video effectively in your presentations.

The Benefits of Using Video

As powerful as still images are, there is often nothing like video to show problems in context or illustrate solutions. For environmentalists, wildlife scientists, and other researchers and scientists who work in the field, for example, video is an easy and compelling way to document their findings for further analysis and to show them to the public and their colleagues. Businesspeople can use video in their presentations to show new stores or products in action or to show interviews with customers or industry experts. TV news programs use myriad video clips to illustrate and illuminate their stories, and we can, too.

Connect at a visceral level

Recently, I made a presentation to one of my classes regarding the rebuilding efforts in the Tohoku area of Japan. The video I chose was a clip from a small town that showed, in real time, a wall of water entering the town during the tsunami of March 11, 2011. None of my students were directly impacted by the tsunami up north, but they had seen many photos of the aftermath since the event, and they undoubtedly were shocked when they first saw the news clips of the natural disaster the day of the event and for several days after.

Before I played the short clip, I showed photos that I took of the recovery process—some images of remarkable destruction but also of amazing resilience on the part of the people rebuilding. Students were interested and paying attention in a rather quiet way, not unusual in Japan. But when the video came up and showed how quickly a tsunami can destroy everything in its path, the demeanor of the students changed. Whereas before they were passively engaged, they were now vocalizing their surprise and shock and amazement out loud. The classroom was now abuzz of chatter and questions, which lead quickly into discussion. This reminded me again of the power of video imagery to hit people at a gut level. The audience already knew intellectually how strong the Tohoku tsunami was, and they had seen photos and perhaps small videos on a smartphone or on YouTube over the years, but when they saw the transformation of a small town right before their eyes on a large screen, it hit them at an emotional level as well. The idea of a 45-foot tsunami is an abstraction to many people. Photos can help illuminate and educate, of course, but video imagery of the phenomenon takes us a little bit closer to being there and touches us more deeply.

Make them feel something

Seth Godin, a marketing guru, says that presentation is about the transfer of emotion. Godin is right. Data and facts are important, but if you are in the business of sharing ideas—and especially if you get on a stage to do so—then you are in the business of communication, and communication includes more than logic and argument. Communication involves empathy, persuasion, and even inspiration. Communication, then, involves emotion.

I have long known that motion pictures—in the form of video for presentations—have a special ability to move people emotionally. A couple of years ago I was reminded just how powerful motion pictures can be at touching us in unexpected ways. As a result, I shared this story at TEDxKyoto in 2011 (you can find the recording at tedxtalks.ted.com). In June of 2010, my mother passed away with me at her bedside. I am the youngest of four sons and was very close to my mom. After her passing I began going through old photos of her life. Photos are wonderful, but then I remembered that there was an old box of 8mm film, home movies that my grandmother used to take. This box was in Oregon, but I had it sent to Japan and took the film to the camera store to be digitized. I took one reel at a time just in case something went wrong. This film is fragile and irreplaceable. The first DVD I got back contained 18 minutes from my mom and dad's wedding in Portland, Oregon, in 1947, less than two years after the end of World War II. I did not know this film existed or that my folks had access to a movie camera in 1947.

Like Howard Hughes in the movie *The Aviator,* I sat alone in the center of our dark home movie theater in Nara, Japan, watching for the first time a beautiful ceremony between 19-year-old versions of my mother and father. These movies have no sound. Just 24 pictures a second giving the illusion of movement. This is when I realized how powerful motion pictures can be. The photographs of my parents' wedding are fun to look at, and they evoke nostalgia. But I could tell from the tears streaming down my face that seeing my parents move and communicate their happiness through their body language was hitting me at a deeper level than I expected. The photos made me smile but the digitized 8mm film footage made me cry and then made me laugh out loud as I shared in their joy some 64 years later and an ocean away. Video has the power to make us feel.

Below are a few of the slides I used in the TEDxKyoto talk. The slide resolution for the presentation was 1280 x 720 (16:9) for the wide screen at TEDxKyoto. However, the resolution for the video clips I had was not as large as the slide. The clips were also at a 4:3 aspect ratio, which was the aspect ratio for 8mm film. Therefore, I decided to keep the video images smaller, and I got around the 4:3 aspect ration by making them look like photographs or like film being projected onscreen. Because the actual screen in the hall was huge, the video was still easy to see.

Here, I begin with what appears to be a photograph of my mother on her wedding day. I talk about the power of the photograph to evoke bittersweet feelings and the like.

The audience assumes it is a photo, but then I silently click the remote in my right hand and that still image comes to life in the form of video. The audience gasps.

This is the footage that hit me so hard when I saw it for the first time, alone at home, on the big screen. As the footage plays during the presentation, I narrate over the silent video clip.

We go from tears to having a laugh. My father and his dad joke around about whether they should give each other a kiss on the lips as they did with my mom and grandma. As you see in the slide on the next page, the answer was yes.

While watching this play out for the first time, I laughed out loud. Every time I show this to an audience today, they laugh out loud, too, even though they do not know my dad. This gives us more evidence of the power of video to evoke emotion.

Who would have thought on that day in 1947 in Portland, Oregon, that the youngest of their yet-to-be-born children would see this 8mm film for the first time in Japan via something called a MacBook Air and a Mitsubishi projector, 64 years after the movie was filmed.

So how did I do it? It's very straightforward. The image above is a screenshot of my Keynote file in slide view with the slide elements moved out a bit to let you see what's in there. As you can see, there are only seven different design elements (not including the black background): Four pieces of tape, one video, and a vintage-looking photograph border to make it seem like a snapshot rather than a movie. (The image of the border is a PNG file with everything except the white border transparent.) The final design element is the background I made in Photoshop, combining some old-style film elements to create a vintage feel. The frame sits on top of the video and the tape elements (also PNG files with some transparency to give the feel of real tape) are placed on top of the frame on the corners.

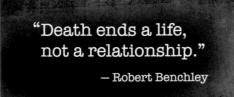

Discovering these old home movies made me feel more than nostalgic—it transported me back in time to when my mother and father were still alive. When I watch the video, it feels like they are not dead. Something is very much alive. Is that just the memories? I suppose. But the emotional impact these simple videos had on me made realize that the old Robert Benchley chestnut is true: Death ends a life, but the relationship lives on. The slide below left features a short clip of my father holding me on my first birthday in 1962. Videos like these really are a kind of emotion generator.

Here, you can see the three elements (not including the black background) that make up the slide. The video is on the bottom. The image of the movie projector (a PNG file) is on top of the video (the screen area is transparent so that the video shows through). Then, the filmic image I used on the background is placed on top for a different effect. The image has a lot of transparency except around the edges.

Change the pace

Video can provide a welcome change of pace in a presentation. For longer presentations, it's especially important to change up what you are doing. There is evidence that people's attention really drops after about ten minutes. Unless you change some aspect of your presentation delivery from time to time, you are going to lose some of your audience. You cannot simply keep talking and dishing out new information. You must do something that is relevant to your topic—something that re-engages your audience or illustrates and supports your point in a *different* way. You can tell a story, give examples, explain a graph, show an illustration or photo, ask a question, and so on. And, of course, using video that relates to your point is also a great way to change pace and engage the viewer's brain, bringing them deeper into your presentation.

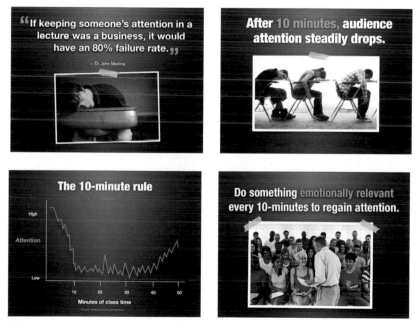

Slides adapted from *Brain Rules* by John Medina.

Other uses for video

A video can give people an "aha moment"—that moment when they clearly realize what was still not clear with words alone. In my experience, a video clip is great for showing a problem or a paradox or highlighting salient points of a controversial issue. The video stimulates greater involvement and encourages people to discuss an issue or ask questions. Here are some more uses of video in a live, short-form presentation:

- **Show a real example.** Something like the effect of an oil spill on local wildlife can be an abstraction until you see it. Photos help support your message, but video allows you to bring the issue right to people in a more direct manner than static images. You want to show a customer who has difficulty opening your newly designed package? A video clip of an actual frustrated customer tells the story much more clearly than photos or words alone.

- **Take them there.** Photos help tell a story, but seeing video clips taken by the presenter feels more like taking a journey to the actual location with the presenter. The issue seems more vivid when we are "there."

- **Show an interview.** There is nothing like good clips from people—experts, customers, people on the ground during a recovery project—who can give us a unique POV (point of view) on an issue. Quotes appearing as text are effective to a degree, but hearing firsthand from those most closely involved in the issue resonates more deeply.

- **Use testimonials.** If you are selling something, statements from actual customers can be effective, but you need to be careful to keep them short. Too many testimonials, or ones that are too long, can make it seem like the presentation is all about you and not about the audience.

- **Show a skit or demonstration.** Show a clip of an emergency procedure, make your own skit of how to handle harassment in the workplace, and so on.

- **Show a transformation over time.** Show the construction of a building over a two-year period, a sped-up video of the great change between high tide and low tide, and so on.

The type of things we can show in a video to engage, illustrate, and make things clear and more memorable to the audience are limited only by our imaginations and the time we need to find or create the video content (no small thing).

Tips for Using Video

Too often, the presenter does not smoothly transition to showing a video clip—at all. Instead, the presenter usually spends a few awkward moments searching for the file and opening the video in a separate application rather than smoothly within the slideware. You've been there. It goes something like this: "OK, let me just show you a video that is a good example of XYZ in action…. OK, um, let me just exit PowerPoint and open my video player… (crickets, crickets…). Where is it? Oh, here it is. Oops, that's my son's graduation ceremony…. Let's see, here it is, XYZ. Now I will just scroll to where the good part is. Um, where is that? Here it is (click). Um, oops, no sound? OK, here it is. Is it too loud? Can you hear it? Let's start that video again. Where's that window? Oh, here it is. And blah, blah, blah." You get the idea. When video is used well, the clips simply become part of the presentation, serving to amplify your content and your connection with the audience without any clumsy hiccups.

Insert the video

Whenever possible, use your slideware's Insert Video/Sound option to embed the video. (In PowerPoint, make sure to put your video files in the same folder as your PowerPoint file.) The advantage of having the video on your hard drive and inserted into your file is that the presentation is smoother. Your videos will just appear when you want, in sync with your narrative, just like the other visuals. Leaving the application to show a video is distracting and visually disruptive. In a good presentation, nobody is aware of your software (or the desktop photo of your cat). They are engaged with you and your media—with your content and story.

In slideware applications such as Keynote, PowerPoint, and Prezi, you can either (1) link to a video online so that it plays in a slide when connected to the Internet or (2) insert the video into your slide from an original video file on your hard disk. I understand that teachers and students often link to online sources such as YouTube when they present at school. That's great…until the video doesn't play. For high stakes presentations in business, important short-form talks such as conference presentations, and events like TED/TEDx, Ignite, and WikiStage, I highly recommend that you *insert* the video from your hard drive. Too many times I have seen presentations get derailed when the video from the Internet did not load because the WiFi was down, the video was removed from the website, or for other inexplicable reasons. When legally possible to do so, it is far better to download the video to your hard disk. Some websites, such as www.ted.com, allow you to download videos in various sizes. You can then insert the video and play the appropriate section inside your presentation. In the slideware you can choose where the video will begin and end.

Below is a screenshot of Keynote in slideview (or navigator view). In the slide I placed a video of bamboo swaying in the wind. The video has a stylistic border to match the natural, organic theme of the presentation's slides. Notice the Inspector at right. I click the video and display the QuickTime options, which let me specify how I want the video to play. In this case, I will talk about resilience and bending but not breaking—much like the bamboo does—so I want the bamboo video file to keep looping behind me as I speak. No one will know it is a loop; it will seem like one long video. As you can see, I set the video to begin when I click my remote because I want people to think it is just a still image at first (until the wind begins). For longer videos, you can set where you want the video to start and stop. This is very useful for long videos, such as TED talks, when you just want to show a short segment.

Bamboo goes with the flow.

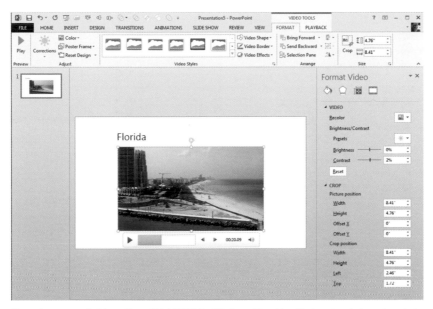

Above is a screenshot from PowerPoint 2013 for Windows. The video file has already been inserted into the slide. (To insert a video from a file, choose Insert on the top left of the ribbon, then choose Video and then Video on My PC. Browse until you find your file and choose Insert.) As you can see here, the Format tab lets you control formatting, including the video size, borders, brightness/contrast, and more.

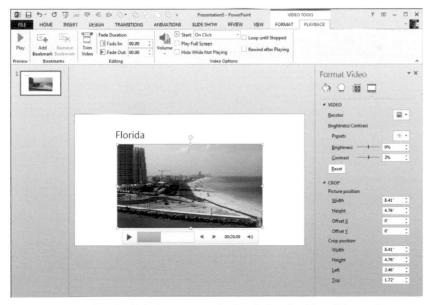

Here, Playback is selected, which gives you several options for how the video will be run. The Trim Video option lets you choose the starting and ending points for the video. You can also loop the video, adjust the audio level, and specify how you want it to start (such as On Click).

Video file from NASA/JPL

Video inserted in slide

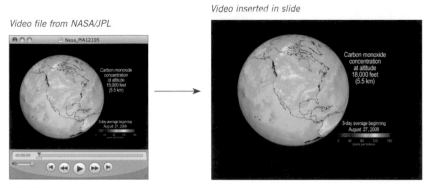

This NASA video animation shows the abundance of carbon monoxide at 18,000 feet over a three-day period. The slide background was set to black to match the background around the animated earth. NASA is an excellent source of multimedia, including video (www.nasa.gov/multimedia).

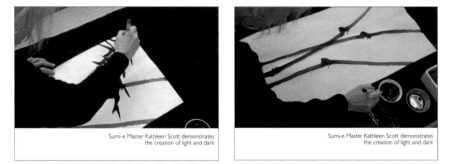

Sumi-e Master Kathleen Scott demonstrates the creation of light and dark

Sumi-e Master Kathleen Scott demonstrates the creation of light and dark

In this video, sumi-e master Kathleen Scott demonstrates the basic brush stroke and how to achieve many colors using only black ink. Because the video is HD, it can fill the slide yet it leaves room below for explanations and terminology to appear on the slide as needed.

In this presentation, as I introduce the term *hadaka no tsukiai* (naked relationship/communication), the text fades in over the top of a video clip of a soothing Japanese *onsen* (hot springs). The movement in the background is smooth and subtle and gently connects the bath and the idea of "naked, we are all the same" to the point of naturalness and honest communication. (Video from iStockphoto.com.)

The smoke billows slowly and dramatically in the background as the text fades in smoothly when the presenter clicks the remote. (Video from iStockphoto.com.)

Video as background

One effective way to use video in a slide presentation is to have it playing in the background while text displays. In this example, the video of factory smoke plays smoothly in the background while text fades in to match a question from the presenter. The text stays onscreen and smoke billows slowly as discussions ensue based on the presenter's question. Throughout the video clip, there is always enough contrast between the background smoke and the text. A drop shadow on the text makes it pop out a bit from the background but in a subtle way.

When the talk turns to alternative sources of energy, this video of slowly rotating windmills plays smoothly in the background as information is introduced. (Video from iStockphoto.com.)

How large should the video be onscreen?

The same principle that applies to type, images, and slides in general applies to video: Make it big enough to see in the back row or don't bother showing the clip. A common complaint when presenters use video is that the video is just too small. Remember when I said not to stretch your photos to make them bigger because that will reduce the quality of of the image? Well, that's still true—but for video, especially high-quality videos that were professionally shot with good light, good compression, etc., you can get away with increasing the size a bit. It's a compromise, of course, but it's better for people in the back to be able to see what's going on even if the quality is somewhat reduced.

Have you ever seen a presenter use a small video like this on a large screen? You would not expect your local theater to show films like this onscreen, and there is no reason for us to make things so hard to see for a presentation audience.

In this version, the video is of a higher resolution and fills the screen. It is not only easy to see the details, but the overall feel is more cinematic and the video has a great deal more impact. When the presenter wants all the attention back on her, the slide can simply fade to black at the appropriate time.

In this hypothetical case, let's say an architect is presenting in her office to potential clients. In her presentation she takes the audience inside some of the firm's current projects. Here, she shows a video of a kitchen still under construction. As the video plays with no sound, she points out the important details of the construction process. Which of these four video sizes makes it easiest for the audience to see the details? Which video has more impact? The slide resolution is 1280 x 720 (16:9). The first slide at the top has a video that is 480 x 270. Pretty small, isn't it?

Here, the video has an aspect ratio that matches the slide (16:9), but it is still very small at only 512 x 288. Can you make out the details?

This is better. The resolution of the video is now 853 x 480. You can increase the screen size of the video in your slideware by pulling on the corners of the video without seeing too much loss of quality. But in this case, we have a larger version of the video, so we do not need to do that (below).

Now the video is full screen. The video was exported from the camera—in this case, an iPhone—in HD 1280 x 720 so it fits perfectly inside the presentation slide.

When presenting on the large stage with a large screen, it is a good opportunity to use visuals that have a big impact on the audience. Here, you can see how silly it would look to show something as dramatic as a space shuttle launch with a small, low-resolution video. The video in the sample at the bottom of the page is the same size as the slide—1280 x 720—and fills the entire screen. Even if your video is not quite the same size as the slide, it may be a good idea to resize the video to play at full screen for a more cinematic effect that is easy for the people in the back row to see.

Many TED presenters make good use of full-screen video during their talks. Above are photos I took of award-winning journalist Jun Hori presenting at TEDxKyoto in 2013. Through his 8bitNews project, Hori plans to lead a newsroom revolution and change the shuttered world of journalism and reporting into a creative and cooperatively shared approach. For his entire talk, HD video played in harmony with his conversational-style narration.

Keep your video clips short

I save this point for last, because it's very important. One of the easiest ways to sabotage your otherwise good presentation is to show video clips that are too long. The general principle is to keep them very short, under 30 seconds. If you show a clip that is a couple of minutes or longer, the audience may begin to lose interest, especially if you do this several times. After all, they came to see and hear you. Of course there are exceptions (and this does not apply to trainers of long seminars), but if you do show, say, a four-minute clip in a 20-minute presentation, make sure you tell people just before you begin the video that it is a four-minute clip.

One of the most common complaints I hear about the ineffective use of video is that the clips are too long. If people *feel* they are too long, the relevance of the clip may need to be questioned in the first place. However, if you are sure that the video clip is vital and helpful for the audience, then make sure you have edited it to make it as short as possible and yet still effective.

Tree-climbing naturalist John Gathright's presentation at TEDxKyoto 2013 was one of the best, most inspiring presentations I've ever seen. He shared a great message with a very dynamic, visual approach.

In Sum

- Try adding video to your presentations for a more engaging experience. Using video related to your point is a great way to change pace and engage the viewer's brain, bringing them deeper into your presentation.

- For high-stakes presentations, linking to clips on the Internet is risky. Whenever possible, insert videos from your hard drive directly into your application.

- Make sure your video clips are big enough to be seen (and heard) from the back of the room. For the most powerful, cinematic effect, fill the screen with the video.

- Video should be as short as possible. In general, unless the video is a long clip that plays behind you as you provide narration, keep the clips to around 30 seconds to one minute.

6

Simplifying the Data

Displaying evidentiary data can be a powerful way to support your case or your discovery. It can also result in tragedy. When people recall their "death-by-PowerPoint" horror stories, their experiences often include the tedium of sitting through pages and pages of detailed charts and graphs without knowing what the displays were supposed to show. The presenter, however, assumed the audience members could see every fine detail from their seats. Audiences quickly tire of data displayed without clarity or meaning, especially when the data is difficult to see. The problem is usually not the use of quantitative data, but rather the way the charts and graphs were created and displayed.

Before you decide to display data onscreen, you need to be clear on its purpose. Is it really necessary for the audience to see absolute numerical precision or do you merely want to show trends and general relationships? In general, especially for presentations to larger audiences, it can be difficult for people to see precise values in graphs. Harvard psychologist Stephen M. Kosslyn clearly makes this point in his book *Graph Design for the Eye and Mind* (Oxford University Press, 2006): "The strong suit of graphs is the illustration of the quantitative relations, and they are not appropriate if you only want to convey precise values. If this is your goal, use a table." As Kosslyn points out, different data and goals require different visual formats. In general, use the formats as follows:

- Tables for specific numbers.
- Graphs, such as bar charts, for complex comparisons.
- Line charts for showing trends.
- Pie charts for comparisons, at least to compare only a few values.

Clarity in Simplicity

Simplicity is a fundamental tenet in all aspects of design and communication. Simplicity is particularly important concerning the creation and display of quantitative information. Most presenters, however, are afraid of simplicity, at least as far as showing data is concerned. Perhaps this is because there exists a fundamental misunderstanding of what it means to be simple today. Many people confuse simple with simplistic—that which is watered down to the point of being deceptive or misleading. To some people, the idea of simplicity means oversimplifying an issue to the point that the presentation ignores complexities and creates obfuscation.

Ancient concepts of the Zen aesthetic still have much to teach us today concerning simplicity. Practical suggestions exist in the *wabi sabi* concept—the aesthetic ideal at the heart of many Zen arts, including *sado* (the way of tea) and *ikebana* (flower arranging). In the book *Wabi Sabi Simple* (Adams Media Corporation, 2004), author Richard Powell offers advice derived from the simplicity of wabi sabi that we can apply to design, including the design of quantitative displays.

> *Do only what is necessary to convey what is essential. In bonsai and in haiku, you prune and trim what is nonessential in an attempt to shorten the distance between the observer and the observed. You carefully eliminate elements that distract from the essential whole, elements that obstruct and obscure.... Clutter, bulk, and erudition confuse perception and stifle comprehension, whereas simplicity allows clear and direct attention.*

If you replaced "bonsai" and "haiku" with "charts" and "graphs" in this passage, it makes good advice for the presenter indeed. That is, we should do only show what is necessary to convey the essential information without excessive ornamentation, clutter, or anything else that gets in the way of clear, direct attention to what's important.

Signal vs. noise

The signal-to-noise ratio (SNR), a term borrowed from radio communications, is a useful way of thinking about simplicity in the creation of charts and graphs. The SNR is easy to understand. If you're old enough, think back to when you used to drive your car while listening to the news on the AM radio. When the broadcast came in loud and clear, you were enjoying a good signal. But when you drove far away from the source, the signal became weaker and the noise—an annoying static—became louder, making the content difficult to hear. Eventually, the static (noise) increased so much that the faint signal and your understanding approached zero. All you wanted was to hear the news, but the low SNR made this impossible.

In the same way, overly complicated, poorly designed charts and graphs have a similar effect on us. Think of the SNR in the visual world as the ratio of relevant to irrelevant elements in a slide or other display.

SNR is a good general principle to keep in mind during all aspects of your design work, but it is especially important to remember when designing quantitative displays for the screen. In the case of charts and graphs, the signal is the concrete message we are trying to show—the data in its clearest form. Visual noise consists of anything that gets in the way of seeing the data—the signal—onscreen in the most direct, clearest way possible. The goal is to have the highest signal-to-noise ratio possible in your slides.

BEFORE

AFTER

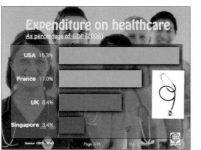
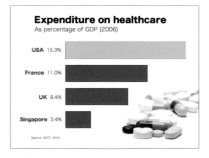

Using one bold color will put the emphasis on that part of the data. Removing the busy background and various colors from the bars helps to add clarity. (Images in slides from iStockphoto.com.)

BEFORE ▼   AFTER ▼

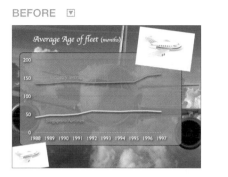 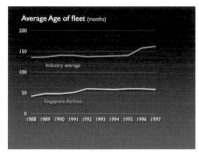

A simple line chart is made unnecessarily noisy with the addition of clip art, a background photo, and a box in a color that does not match the theme.

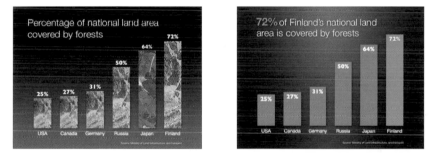

For the most part, I do not recommend using the built-in textures—unless there is a very good reason to do so.

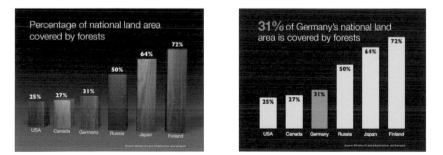

The 3D effect does not look too bad in this case—at least the wood texture has some relation to the content. But as a general rule, avoid 3D effects as they distort the data.

Three principles for presenting data

The kinds of graphs you use in a presentation depend on your unique situation and objectives. The only rule concerning the display of data—besides telling the truth—is simplicity. You can achieve simplicity in the design of effective charts, graphs, and tables by remembering three fundamental principles: restrain, reduce, and emphasize.

Restrain

The hardest thing to do is edit yourself—to stop adding more. It's up to you to make the tough decisions about what to include and what to leave out. Most presenters include too much information in a display. Charts and graphs can be hard enough for the audience to see, so we should be careful not to make it more difficult for them by adding superfluous elements that do more harm than good.

Clutter such as footers, logos, and decorative items obviously create noise. Including too much data—more than is necessary to make your point—can produce noise as well. Your job is to include as much as necessary, but no more. Success fundamentally depends on making good decisions about what to leave in and what to leave out, and this requires you to exercise restraint. Including deep levels of quantitative detail may be inappropriate for projection on a screen, which has relatively low resolution. You might, instead, include detailed data in a handout.

BEFORE ▾   AFTER ▾

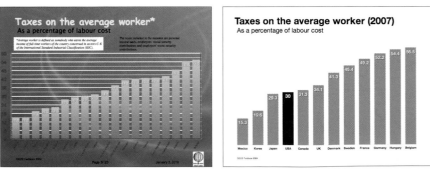

Reduce

Many quantitative displays can become more effective if you simply reduce the nonessential. In his book *The Power of Simplicity* (MIT Press, 2006), John Maeda cites reduction as the first step: "The simplest way to achieve simplicity is through thoughtful reduction," Maeda says. "When in doubt, just remove. But be careful of what you remove." So how do you decide what to remove? By reminding yourself what is important. Ask yourself several questions:

- What will the display really show your audience?
- How will it help them to see your point?
- What is the essence of the point this particular chart helps to make?
- Are any elements in this slide nonessential?

Emphasize

By emphasize I do not mean to exaggerate, spin, or distort the data. What I mean is that we must point to what is important. What is it that you think is most important? What is the most salient point to you? Make this clear to the audience.

There are two simple ways to emphasize what is important in charts and graphs, which makes them easier to understand. The first is to use contrast—such as color—to highlight the part you want people to focus on. The second method is to write a declarative statement rather than a title at the top of the slide. For example: "Reported cases of influenza decreased by 17% in 2009" instantly suggests the meaning of the chart and communicates much more than something like "Reported cases of influenza (2009)."

In the design of quantitative displays, simplicity is our overriding approach. The general principles of restrain, reduce, and emphasize—along with other principles explored in previous chapters—can help us achieve a kind of simplicity that helps the audience understand our point and why it matters.

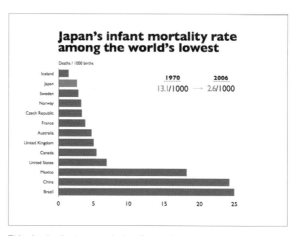

This simple chart uses a declarative sentence and color to emphasize the key point of the slide.

When to Use a Document Instead of Slides

In the spring of 2008, the CEO of Toyota Motor Corporation, Katsuaki Watanabe, urged employees in Japan to stop the wasteful practice of using PowerPoint for the creation of ineffective documents, what I call *slideuments*. Watanabe made this statement during a talk about the need to reduce costs at Toyota. In a reminder to employees to be cost conscious, he cited the use of PowerPoint as an example of waste—a waste of both time and money. To make his case, Watanabe spoke of his early days in the company. Back then, employees used just one piece of paper to make a point, submit a proposal, or summarize an issue. But now, everything is printed from PowerPoint, which uses many sheets of paper and expensive color ink. "It's all wasteful," Watanabe said.

Watanabe was not saying that PowerPoint is necessarily harmful. His point was that printed documents from a presentation tool tend to have less content and less clarity, and yet use more paper, more ink, and more time to produce.

In the context of a challenging economy and an atmosphere of reducing costs, what would you say of any business practice that (1) takes more time, (2) costs more money, and (3) is less effective? In the spirit of *kaizen* (continuous improvement), even if the waste is small, it must be eliminated.

Don't confuse slides with documents

The difference between slides and documents may be obvious to you. But for many people, it is not. Visuals projected onscreen in support of a live talk are very different from material created for print to be read and analyzed. When you hear the term "PowerPoint presentation," you often think of poor usage— dull, hard-to-read slides containing long-winded paragraphs. In the same way, PowerPoint is used to ill effect when you print out reams of tiny slides that lack depth as well as readability, a form of the dreaded slideument.

A common problem is the lack of distinction between documents and presentation slides prepared for projection. They are often seen as being interchangeable, but they are not. Slideuments make understanding and precision harder when printed. And when used as projected slides in a darkened conference room, they are the corporate world's number one cure for insomnia. This is not the fault of PowerPoint or Keynote, however, as slideware is simply a tool. As you've seen, it is a tool that can be used effectively or ineffectively. It all depends on your approach and your particular need.

If you have deep and complex data that is absolutely necessary for your audience to see, then they need time to examine it and maybe refer to it later. If so, then the ephemeral nature of projected slides may not be appropriate. But if you are showing trends or simple, straightforward comparisons of data, then projected slides will work. Consider using a mix of slides and handouts. Many effective presenters use high-quality images and clear, aesthetically pleasing quantitative displays for most of their talk, but on occasion stop to hand out deeper levels of data in printed format. For smaller audiences at conferences and seminars—and certainly for boardrooms   the latter approach can be very effective. (For a new perspective, see Nancy Duarte's "Slidedocs: a primer" on the following page. A Slidedoc is a digital document that has the perfect blend of text along with visual content that is necessarily missing in the slides of a good keynote-style talk. Yet the slidedoc can go deeper than just printing the typical slideuments of yesteryear.)

If you have detailed numbers that people need to spend some time with, it may be better to change gears in your talk and stop to distribute a handout to your audience so that they may better see the data. This not only makes your numbers easier to see and compare, it also provides a change of pace in the talk that will help keep the audience engaged.

Nancy Duarte

CEO, author, presentation pioneer

www.duarte.com

Nancy Duarte is the cofounder and CEO of Duarte, Inc., a presentation development and design company that creates presentations for the world's leading brands and some of the most influential people of our time. She's written several books on presentation design and storytelling, including Resonate, slide:ology, *and the* HBR Guide to Persuasive Presentations.

Slidedocs: a primer

Presentations have the power to move an audience and inspire them to take action. But there are also plenty of circumstances where a formal presentation isn't the best tool for the job.

We know this intuitively. How many times have you heard someone say, "Hey, can you send me your slides?" When somebody asks you this question, what they're really saying is

"I want the information in your presentation, but I don't want you to present it to me."

Presentations are a single point on a larger spectrum of communications, all of which have their own set of uses and best practices. If you're creating an effective presentation, though, there won't be enough information on your slides to fully inform your reader. That's part of what makes it a presentation. The slides support the presenter. They don't replace him. If there really is enough information to understand the material without the help of a presenter, you're probably not creating a presentation; you're creating a document.

But presentation software is such a convenient tool for combining text and visuals that we've been content to live in this limbo where we *read* presentations and *present* documents. Instead, we need a third medium—a medium that combines visuals and text for maximum clarity, allows the reader to digest information quickly, can stand on its own, and is relatively simple to create.

Slidedocs are this new medium. A slidedoc is a document, created in presentation software, that deftly combines text and visuals for maximum understanding. Slidedocs accommodate how we communicate today—in short bursts like texts or Tweets. Plus, they give us the flexibility to pair words with pictures without having to learn sophisticated publishing software.

Slidedoc

Presentation

Here are some situations where slidedocs are most useful:

Emissary
You can't be there, but you still want to get your information across.

Pre-read
You want to start a group conversation with a shared base of knowledge.

Reference Material
You want to give people something to look at more closely and at their own pace.

Follow-up Material
You need to explain the "what" and the "how" after a presentation.

Slidedocs are a great tool because the medium capitalizes on something many of us are doing already: using presentation software to capture our brightest thoughts even when we aren't presenting. But how do we do it effectively?

Slidedocs are meant to be read. So, in order to create an effective slidedoc, it makes sense to take some tips from print. If you look at some of your favorite print publications, you'll realize they include some standard practices that help you consume the information at both the page and the document level.

Page-level Hierarchy

Headlines
6-to-10-word titles around the slide's main topic

Subheads
Includes the thesis or a summary of the slide's main point

Body copy
Full sentences that make up paragraphs of complete thoughts

Pull quotes
To emphasize important points (either inline or repeated in box)

three column text layout

With subtitle placeholder

Lorem ipsum dolor sit anamet, conse ctetur adipisicing elit, sed do eiusmod and estempor incididunt ut labore et dolore magna aliqua. Ut enimeys and minim veniam, quis nostrud antine commodo consequat.

Duis aute irure dolor indiduen reprderit in voluptate velit esse cillum dolore eu fugiat nulla pariatur. Excepteur didu the int occaecat cupidatat an esnon. deser espn and the unt mollit anim id est and

laborum. At vero eos minus id quod et accusamus et iusto odio dignissimos ducimus.

And tatum deleniti didu atque corrupti quos dolores et quas molestias excepturi didu thint occaecati cuditate non and the lorem ipsum dolor and the deserunt and harum quidem rerum esfacilis est et expedita distinctio. Nam libero tempore, cum an soluta nobis est oligondi and epoptio cumque nihil and impedit quo minus id

quod the maxime placeat facere didu the eos et the ollitia animi, id est lorem ipsum laborum et ates and the repan and this ddolorum fuga est and accpossimu.

Call out any important messages. Keep it short.

section 03

Cover

Section Breaks

Glossary

Table of Contents

Slidedoc Architecture

Cover
A snappy title paired with some nice visual elements will get your Slidedoc read.

Table of Contents
A Slidedoc of any length requires a simple way to find what you need.

Section Breaks
A transitional page that uses a bold color, graphics, or memorable type to signify the changing of a topic.

Glossary and/or Index
Include a glossary and/or index for easy reference and navigation.

When something can be read without effort, great effort has gone into its writing.

— Enrique Jardiel Poncela

Writing for a Slidedoc

A slidedoc is the perfect place to put detailed information, but you still have to be concise. First, you don't have as much real estate as you would in a document. Second, slidedocs are meant to be consumed relatively quickly. Your goal should be one idea per slide.

So, take the time to really craft your words. You'll need to use complete sentences because your slidedoc will travel on its own, but make sure each sentence counts.

The above slides show what can be accomplished with a simple grid and supporting diagram. Notice how much more inviting the bottom example is.

Designing a Slidedoc

Because slidedocs have dense content, it's more important than ever to lay out that content with purpose.

Grids give you a structure from which to hang your images and text and keep your layouts tidy. Grids also help you organize text into columns, which makes it easier for your audience to read your information.

Include data, but avoid unnecessary decoration. Make it easy for readers to discern what you're trying to say by highlighting your main takeaway.

Let your content breathe with white space. It'll help people focus on what's important.

The flexibility of slidedocs releases people to be agile communicators—presenting information when necessary and allowing audiences to read when it's not.

Slidedocs are easy to throw together quickly. But easy doesn't give us license for laziness. Regardless of the vehicle you use to communicate your message, putting in the time to create good work always wins.

Common Charts and Graphs

Myriad graphs can be used, depending on the data you want to show. Regardless of the type of graph you use or how much detail you need to show, the principle is always the same: Make it as clear as possible. Let's look at just a few of the more common types of charts and graphs used in business and academia.

Pie charts

Pie charts show the relative size of parts to the whole. They are perhaps the most used—and the most misused—of all graphical displays. The problem with pie charts is that we are not very good at accurately gauging the differences in size among the slices. If the size difference is very small, it is nearly impossible.

In addition, if you have many values, the slices become so thin that the pie chart format becomes impractical. In this case, it is better to use a bar graph. Many researchers avoid pie charts altogether. While pie charts may not be as good as bar charts for accurately displaying differences among values, what pie charts have going for them is familiarity. When you do use pie charts, keep the following things in mind:

- No 3-D effects.

- No legend—put labels inside or next to the chart.

- Highlight what's important.

BEFORE   AFTER

Bar graphs

Bar graphs are good for showing comparisons among values. The bars may be horizontal or vertical. Vertical bar charts, also called column charts, are good for displaying values across a category. When the number of variables across the x-axis becomes large, however, it is difficult to label them in a manner that can be easily seen from the audience (without setting the labels at an angle). In this case, a horizontal bar chart may offer more room for writing the labels clearly.

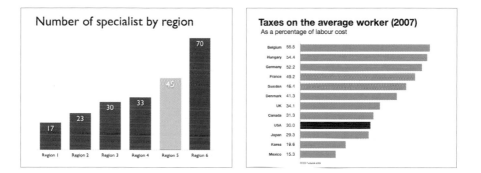

Stacked bar graphs

A stacked bar graph is useful for displaying the whole and its parts over multiple instances. Emphasis is on the whole, but you can get a sense of the part in relation to the whole in each instance.

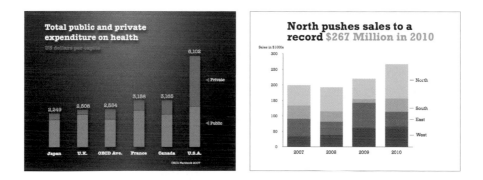

Divided-bar graphs

A divided bar graph shows parts of a whole. Some people prefer divided bar graphs to pie charts because we are not very accurate at determining the area of a circle. If there are many small variables, the divided-bar graph *may* be easier to understand than a pie chart (though a regular bar chart is easier still).

Scatter plots

Scatter plots are useful for showing a general relationship between two variables and an overall impression of the relationship.

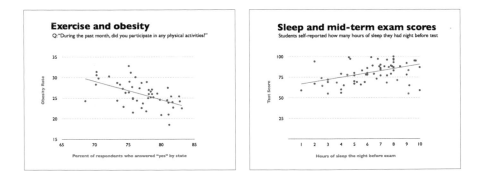

Line graphs

Line graphs are good at showing trends over time. Use a line graph if the x-axis is an interval scale such as days, weeks, or months.

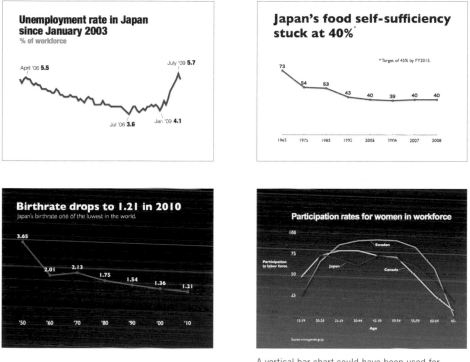

A vertical bar chart could have been used for this, but the goal was to show the trend and the shape of the data rather than the numbers. Here you can see the "M-curve" in the case of Japan. Many women in Japan drop out of the workforce when they have children (and then re-enter the workforce again later).

What About Picture Graphs?

Picture graphs use visuals to represent the data points. They are very common in popular media because they get your attention—at least that's the idea. While I am a fan of high-impact visuals, I am not crazy about picture graphs. The downside is that they (1) take longer to create and (2) can obscure the actual data. But the primary reason I avoid picture graphs is simply because graphs themselves—if designed well—are already powerful visuals. There is no reason to decorate the data with pictures.

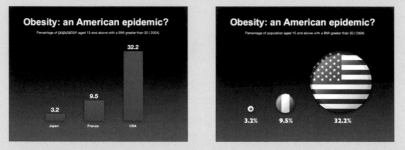

In general, our visual perception is not very good at accurately comparing areas of a circle. The chart on the right also greatly exaggerates the data—the area of the American flag bubble is far larger than ten times the Japanese bubble.

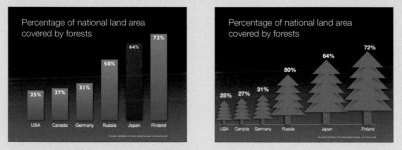

Our visual perception is pretty good at seeing differences in line length in a bar chart, but this is made more difficult with the irregular shape and exaggerated area of the illustrated trees.

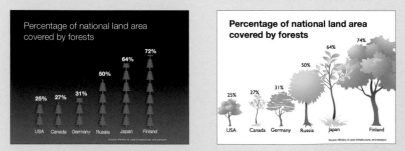

Both of these versions distort the data—especially the slide on the right, which takes much more time to make than a simple bar chart. The slide on the right is appealing, but does not help the viewer see or remember the percentages among the six nations used.

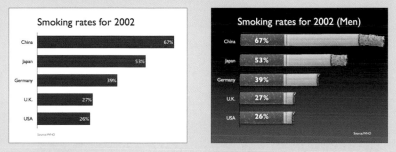

Although I prefer the simpler chart, this picture graph does not distort the numbers (the bar for China is too long, but the end burns off to become the appropriate length).

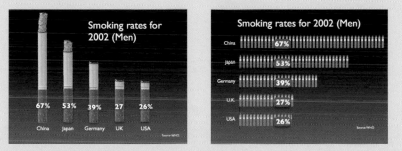

These are different variations of the idea of using pictures in place of simple lines or bars. Even though the data is very simple, it takes more work to understand the numbers.

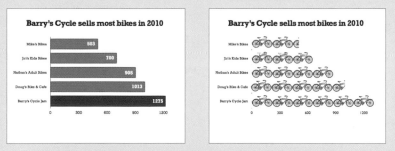

The numbers in this simple bar chart are easy to read quickly, but the numbers become harder to see when a picture graph is used to show the same information. (Images in slides from iStockphoto.com.)

You can always recognize truth by its beauty and simplicity.

— Richard Feynman, physicist

Stephen Few's Graph Design IQ Test

Stephen Few is a leading authority in the field of data visualization and business intelligence. Through his company, Perceptual Edge, he focuses on the effective analysis and presentation of quantitative business information. Few is a remarkable presenter and a highly sought-after speaker, trainer, and consultant. He is the author of several books on data information visualization, including the second edition of his bestseller, *Information Dashboard Design: Displaying Data for At-a-Glance Monitoring* (Analytics Press, 2013). Here, Few shares his Graph Design IQ Test, which is also available on his Web site. This quiz is very straightforward, but the important thing is to know why one design is better than the other—and to be able to articulate the difference.

You can find a Flash version of this Graph Design IQ Test on the Perceptual Edge Web site (and you can check your answers there as well).

www.perceptualedge.com

1. Which graph makes it easier to determine whether Mid-Cap U.S. Stock or Small-Cap U.S. Stock has the greater share?

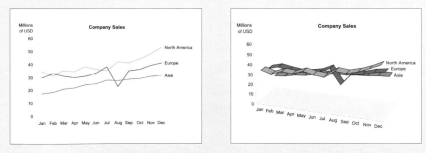

2. Which of these line graphs is easier to read?

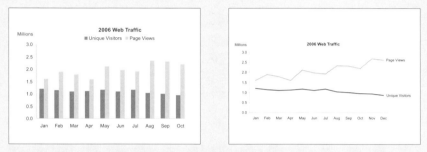

3. Which of these two tables is easier to read?

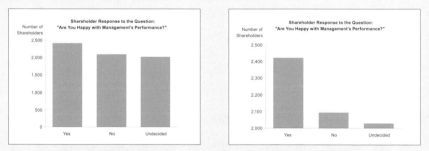

4. Which graph makes it easier to focus on the pattern of change through time, instead of the individual values?

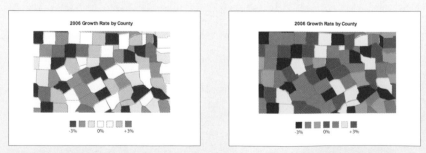

5. Only one of these graphs accurately encodes the values. The other skews the values in a misleading manner. Which graph presents the data accurately?

6. Which map makes it easier to find all of the counties with positive growth rates?

7. Which graph makes it easier to determine R&D's travel expense?

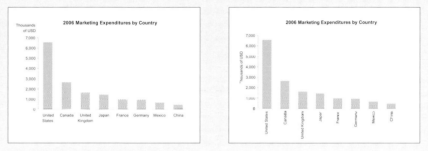

8. In which graph are the labels easier to read?

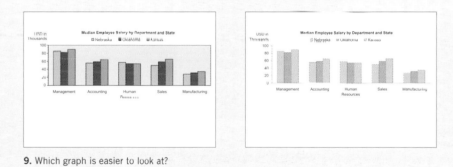

9. Which graph is easier to look at?

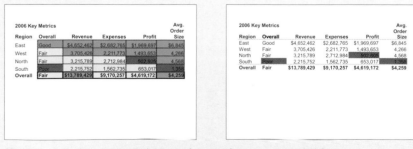

10. Which table allows you to see the areas of poor performance more quickly?

The Future of Data Presentation

One of the masters of displaying data during live presentations is Hans Rosling, a public health professor from the Karolinska Institutet in Stockholm, Sweden. With his amazing ability to unveil the beauty of statistics, Rosling has become a bit of a super star. His talks during the annual Technology, Entertainment, Design (TED) Conferences have been seen online millions of times. In an interview with Paul Miller of the Cloud Computing Podcast, Rosling claims that good data can tell a story, but it is up to us—the presenters—to let this story out. It is up to us to show it in a way that connects with an audience. The data, he says, are like musical notes that must be played to be truly appreciated.

> *...few people will appreciate the music if I just show them the notes. Most of us need to listen to the music to understand how beautiful it is. But often that's how we present statistics: We just show the notes, we don't play the music.*

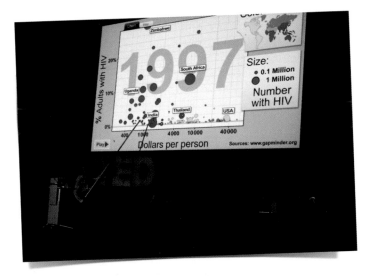

Hans Rosling gets involved with the data at TED 2009 in Long Beach, California.

Let your data speak

As a presenter, what sets Rosling apart is his animation of the data. Before Gapminder, he had been using data and playing it beautifully—in fact, he was a bit of a hero in his own academic community. But it was the Gapminder software that allowed him to really connect with people—to reveal the meaning of data and tell a story to the greater public. What was missing before was the "instrument of playing," says Rosling. Gapminder, which allows for complex animation, provides that instrument. "In statistics we need the composers, we need people who make the instruments, and we need those who play."

Gapminder was founded in Stockholm by Ola Rosling, Anna Rosling Rönnlund, and Hans Rosling in early 2005. Trendalyzer, the Gapminder software, makes it possible to unveil the beauty of a statistical time series by converting "boring numbers" into engaging, animated, and interactive graphics. You can use the online Trendalyzer software in the form of Gapminder World, a Web service that displays a time series of development statistics for all countries (Google acquired Trendalyzer from the Gapminder Foundation in 2006).

Gapminder World

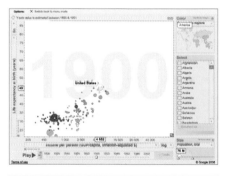

Gapminder World is loaded with more than 200 indicators displaying trends as far back as the year 1800 in some cases. Gapminder World is an amazing tool that is especially useful for educators or anyone else who is interested in seeing the beauty of statistics. Pictured here are two screen shots of the interface. Gapminder World is extremely easy to use and able to illuminate large amounts of data in a simple, clear, and highly visual way.

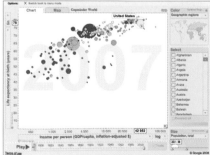

In this example you have Income per Person on one axis and Life Expectantcy (an indicator of health) on the other axis. The size of the bubbles represents population. Through the magic of animation, you can see how the variables change over time, presenting you with a clear picture of the data. Go to Gapminder to experiment with the data yourself.

www.gapminder.org/world

According to Rosling, a good example of professionals who have learned to present (play) data to the public in a visual, direct, clear way are TV meteorologists. Basically, they animate the weather. We can learn a lot from meteorologists, says Rosling, "especially when you consider how many millions of data points they start out with. If meteorologists tried to teach the public how to interpret their raw data, they would have failed. But instead they discovered that some of them could summarize the data in graphics and others were good at talking about the visualization of the data."

Today, data displayed with slideware such as PowerPoint and Keynote is pretty static. Generally, the only animation you see is simple reveals of layers or the introduction of text elements in sync with the speaker. In the future, I hope to see more animation of data—animation that allows "the data to sing" and become more meaningful and memorable. Organizations such as Gapminder (www.gapminder.org) and companies such as Tableau Software (www.tableausoftware.com) are already creating tools that make it possible for presenters to animate data and display it quickly in ways that amplify the meaning, engage the audience, and make things clear and memorable. There are simply no more excuses to be dull. Do not simply display data—present the data so that its story is revealed to all.

In Sum

- Aim for the highest signal-to-noise ratio (SNR) as possible in your slides. In the case of charts and graphs, the signal is the concrete message we are trying to show—it's the data in its clearest form. Visual noise consists of anything that gets in the way of seeing the data—the signal—in the most direct, clearest way possible.

- Simplicity is a fundamental tenet in all aspects of design and communication. It is especially important concerning the creation and display of quantitative information. You can achieve it in the design of effective charts, graphs, and tables by remembering three fundamental principles: restrain, reduce, and emphasize.

- Don't confuse slides with documents. If you have deep and complex data that is absolutely necessary for your audience to see, then create handouts that they can refer to later. If you are showing trends or simple, straightforward comparisons of data, then projected slides will work best.

- There are many different ways to display data. Choose the chart or graph type that works best for your information with the goal of making it as clear as possible.

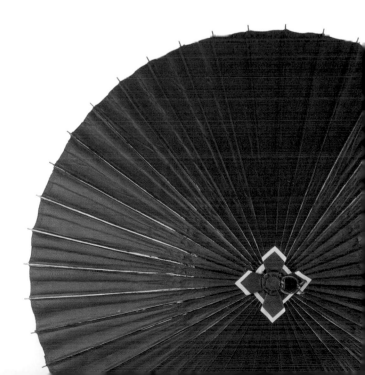

principles

Negative space is magical—
create it, don't just fill it up!

—Timothy Samara,
graphic designer
and educator

7

Seeing and Using Space

To many people, a slide—or a document or a Web page—is something to fill with content. The more content the better, because it shows that you did your homework. Many people do not really think about "space," except when they notice a blank spot being "wasted." The challenge is to think differently about visuals. Learn to see space in a different way and use it effectively in your own presentations.

Empty space, generally referred to as "white space" whether or not it's white, is just as valuable as positive design elements, such as images and text. Space is not just something to be filled in; it is itself a valuable tool for achieving engaging, clear visual messages. White space can help direct the viewer's eyes to positive elements by providing a contrasting quiet area that naturally "points" toward positive elements. White space is necessary for creating designs with balance, harmony, and clear hierarchy.

If you use white space as much as other elements in your visuals, you've taken the first step toward avoiding visual clutter and confusion. When we encounter cluttered visuals, it is natural for the eyes to quickly lose interest or tire. For high-quality printed materials, documents can be far more visually dense since readers can scan, examine, and explore at their own pace. Yet, even graphics and text in printed material must make liberal and intentional use of white space, with the readability of surrounding text as the foremost goal in the designer's mind. For visuals projected onscreen to augment a live talk, however, the careful, thoughtful use of white space is crucial. All the challenges that arise in a live-presentation setting—such as poor lighting, various viewing angles, and so on—can be mitigated with the use of white space in the slide composition.

The Beauty and Function of Space

Why do visual novices fill slides with so much text and so many images? Part of the problem is that we must first learn to see space. This practice seems to be lacking in our education. I often receive email messages on this topic from students from different parts of the world. They, too, believe that presentations should be highly visual—that the words should come from the mouth of the presenter in a natural and engaging way, and not repeated in long lines of text in slides. Yet, these students claim that instructors discourage them from presenting in any manner that deviates from the "normal" noisy approach.

Recently, a student told me that his professor said he did a great job with his research and presentation, but his presentation was graded down because some of the information from the live talk was not repeated in bulleted form on the slides. Presenting effectively sometimes means going against conventional wisdom—the same conventional wisdom that says seven or so lines of text on slide after slide is an acceptable approach. It takes courage to be different and allow white space to remain on a slide.

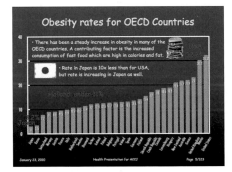

The first slide on the left is a conventional slide, which has clutter and hard-to-see data. The slide on the bottom left is simpler and focused on comparing only Canada with the highest and lowest rated countries for obesity. A handout could be given with all the countries listed if deemed nessary. A paper handout is more helpful when you need to compare lots of numbers. The empty space then allows for the placement of a visual (bottom right) that supports the narrative of the talk.

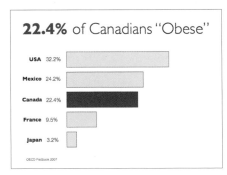

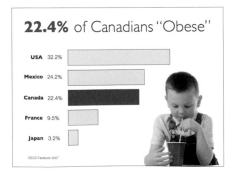

What is space?

If you take an empty slide and put even a single word on it, you have created "space." Before you place anything on a slide, it is just a frame filled with possibilities. Once you add an element, you activate the space. Space can help illuminate a topic, guide a viewer, and achieve harmony. Or, space can be wasted, neglected, and treated like an afterthought. Beginners focus only on the figures—positive elements such as text and numbers, graphs, and labels— without realizing that the secret to a well-designed slide is white space.

Many designers claim that their work actually consists of arranging the white space to bring the positive elements alive in the clearest way possible. White spaces are themselves shapes, like the silent spaces between notes that give jazz its rich form of expression, for example. Without the silent "shapes" and patterns, music would be just intolerable noise.

Without space, you're dead

The legendary graphic designer Paul Rand once said, "Without contrast you are dead." He's right. Contrast is indeed fundamental to good design, and without white space, good contrast cannot be achieved. The leading cause of the lack of contrast is clutter. Too many layers of visual complication make contrast weak, if it even exists. White space allows for real differences to be created, emphasized, and noticed. Space allows for elements—such as text, images, and lines—to breathe. Just like life itself, it is this invisible breath that sustains and empowers. In this sense, then, we can say that without space, you are (also) dead. Embrace empty space.

Embrace empty space

Image in slide from NASA.

Ikebana and Space

The Japanese perception of beauty is largely based on space, especially space as it is found in nature (although that may not seem obvious standing in the bustling center of Shibuya or Shinjuku in Tokyo). Once you understand the importance of space, the intricacies of Japanese art and design begin to make sense. In the case of *ikebana*—the traditional Japanese art of flower arrangement—space is a central component of the floral design. One who practices ikebana sees space not as something to fill in or use, but rather as an element to be created, preserved, and respected. Proper use of space allows the positive elements in the piece to form rhythmical lines that flow, engaging the viewer with the composition. An ikebana artist learns to leave room between the branches to allow a figurative breeze to pass through and rustle the branches, just as would occur in the natural world.

The Japanese word for the type of space employed in Japanese art forms—such as the traditional Japanese garden, *ikebana,* and *sumi-e*—is *ma* (間). Ma is what allows for implied movement in a composition. Ma allows the space for harmonious relationships to form. Think of ma as the void or pause that gives shape to the whole. Lack of space, on the other hand, leads to clutter and disharmony.

To those unfamiliar with the art of ikebana, it may seem like a casual craft with no formal rules. In fact, there are clear rules governing the art of ikebana, depending on the category of the arrangement. The rules are based on solid design principles and centuries of keen observation of nature by the ikebana masters. While there is a formality governing line, form, materials, and so on, there is great room for creativity within the structure of the rules.

As with all traditional Japanese arts, lessons are hidden within that we can apply to our own work and to our own lives, in and out of the design sphere. Read on for a few of the ikebana rules.

10 design lessons from ikebana

1. Space is as important as positive elements. Learn to see space.
2. Space allows other elements to "breathe" and connect.
3. Empty space is a powerful amplifier, helping create a whole that is more engaging than the mere sum of the individual parts.
4. Suggestion and subtlety in design engage the viewer, allowing them to complete the uncompleted.
5. Arrangements (designs) should stimulate the imagination of the viewer.
6. In formality there exists creativity and freedom of expression. No structure, no freedom.
7. In simplicity there exists clarity, beauty, and meaning.
8. Asymmetrical balance is natural, dynamic, and engaging.
9. For the designer (or artist), focus, calm, gentleness, and vision are more important qualities than raw enthusiasm. Slow down your busy mind.
10. Careful arrangement of the elements based on solid principles creates beauty and engagement without decoration.

An appreciation for asymmetrical balance is considered by many to demonstrate a capacity for higher-order thinking.

— Matthew Frederick, architect

Achieving Balance in Space

Balance is a natural part of life. Physically, we need a balanced diet and a good balance of exercise and rest. We seek balance in our personal and professional lives. (We even have a term—work/life balance—that underscores our deep desire for it.) We can also sense when things are not balanced. Say that you walk into a house you're thinking of buying, and you feel that the floors are uneven and then notice that the beams are not perfectly straight, and so on. That lack of balance might affect your purchasing decision. In music, we seek a balance among the parts that work together in harmony to form good sounds. Even if the notes are played correctly, if there is no balance in volume among the instruments, the quality suffers and the audience notices. When things are not in balance, we notice it.

In graphic design, we also seek balance. Balance among the parts contributes to harmony and keeps the viewer engaged. Balanced elements help activate negative space and guide the viewer's eyes around the design. An imbalanced design may get attention, but the discord among the elements will be ineffective for guiding the eyes, thereby limiting the quality of the message. Balance in a design also creates a sense of depth and movement, which prevents the visual from feeling static.

Symmetry

Symmetry occurs when both halves of a design are more or less similar. Essentially, there are two types of symmetry.

- *Rotational symmetry* occurs when elements appear to rotate out from the center. This type of symmetry can be rather dynamic, but it is harder to employ effectively.

- *Bilateral symmetry*, the most common type of symmetry used for slides, is achieved by arranging the left and right sides of a visual to be virtually identical. This kind of symmetry evokes feelings of stability and formality, an effect that may be desirable.

When you center a title and four lines of text in a slide—and center the logo at the bottom—you have created a symmetrical slide. It may be balanced on each side, but it is also static. Symmetry is not bad, but centering all the elements on a slide often leads to dead or wasted space around the edges.

Asymmetry

Asymmetry—or asymmetrical balance—occurs when contrasting elements are arranged in such a way that the weight of the whole visual still appears balanced. The white space in an asymmetrically balanced visual is activated and plays a key role in allowing the positive elements to play off each other in a harmonious and balanced way. Asymmetrical balance among elements of different sizes, weights, colors, etc., is an effective way to guide viewers through a design.

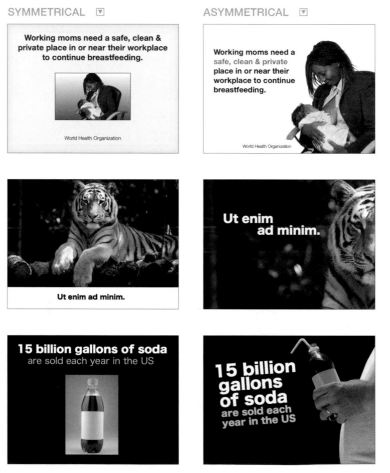

Images in slides from iStockphoto.com.

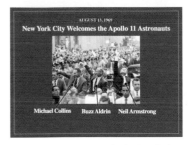

The slides above are not bad, though they are common and lack impact. Elements on the slide are more or less centered and don't have a strong design. (Images in slides from NASA.)

Here, the images in the slides are larger and both the type treatment and image work together to create more of a visual impact. The image will get your attention first, but the type pops out as well.

Visual center

The human eye is pretty good at spotting the vertical center of a visual. If the vertical center is just slightly off, a design may not look quite right. The rulers and guides in slideware allow you to perfectly center objects on the vertical axis. For this reason (and many others), it's a good idea to display the rulers while you are working. For centering elements along the horizontal axis, however, it is acceptable to use your eye. The bottom half of a visual needs more weight, so if you center objects perfectly on the horizontal axis according to the rulers, it will actually seem a bit too low. This is why, for example, in many typefaces the number 8 and the capital S are usually a little fatter on the bottom.

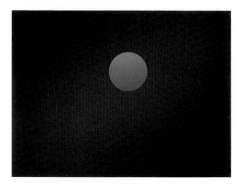

It's easy to see when something is just slightly off vertical center. Use the grids/rulers in your slideware to get the vertical center perfect (assuming that is your intention).

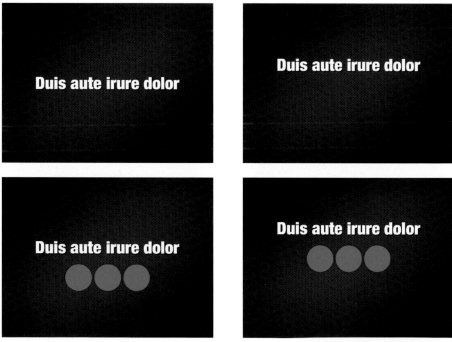

The elements in the two slides above are aligned with the center horizontal axis, but seem just a bit too low.

Here greater visual weight is placed below the elements, resulting in a more balanced feel.

Mind the edges

Most people pay little attention to the edges of visuals, but this space matters as well. Whether you decide to crowd the edges or leave an invisible frame around the edges of slides, the key is to be intentional and consistent. With large photos, they might as well bleed off the edges of slides. If you decide not to fill the entire screen with an image, be sure the invisible frame of white space is wide enough to look intentional and provide breathing space. Personally, I do not see the need for including an actual frame around the slide unless you have a very large screen. Screens are almost always too small, not too large—so why fill valuable white space with a full border or decorative frame?

A consistent border acts as protection around the photographic element. White is clean and dramatic.

A full-screen image is dramatic and allows an interesting interplay between figure (foreground elements) and ground (background). The images lead your eyes to the type. (Images in slides from iStockphoto.com.)

On occasion, it is OK to bleed text or images other than photographs off the edges. But when you place an object so that it almost—but not quite—touches the edges of a slide, it creates an uncomfortable visual effect.

The photo almost bleeds off the edge—was this intentional?

This photo is given a protective border from the edge—looks intentional.

This photo bleeds off just one edge for a more dramatic effect.

This full-screen image has impact and drama but the type looks too close to the edge. Intentional?

Here, the text is given plenty of space and pops out even over a colorful image.

The type bleeds off the edge for a dynamic effect, stressing the point of space (as if the slide is not big enough to hold the large type).

Gestalt and the Power of the Whole

The Gestalt theories of visual perception, developed in Germany in the 1920s, look at the way people naturally seek to simplify visual stimuli by organizing parts and groups into unified wholes. Our brains seek unity and wholeness, so the interaction of the myriad visual elements that comprise a work of art—or a building and so on—contribute to our intuitive interpretation of the whole. Context is a very important consideration in the Gestalt principles of perception. It is the relationship of the elements, not the individual elements themselves, that we see in the whole.

Gestalt theories of perception involve a complex field of study. For our purposes, however, it is useful to know the general idea of "Gestalt" because many of the ideas can help you better understand how to approach the design of slide elements.

According to Merriam-Webster's definition, Gestalt is "a structure, configuration, or pattern of physical, biological, or psychological phenomena so integrated as to constitute a functional unit with properties not derivable by summation of its parts." You have probably heard the saying that "the whole is greater than the sum of its parts." This is an oversimplification of Gestalt, yet it's a reasonable way of recalling the meaning of it. In Japanese, we might say *nantonaku* (this design works). That is, without even investigating the visual details of individual elements to see why a design or piece of art "works," we see that somehow, in its totality, it does indeed seem to communicate well.

The whole is indeed more—sometimes much more—than the sum of the design elements. With music, for example, the total sound that results from the interplay of several musicians is far greater than the sum of the notes being played by all the musicians. Recently, I saw a Tower of Power concert at the Osaka Blue Note. Individually, each musician is world class; some are even legendary. But put them together and they are not just a great band, they are Tower of Power—one of the greatest blues bands ever, with a trademark signature sound. The Gestalt, so to speak, of Tower of Power is far greater, cooler, and more amazing than the totality of its talented individual members. Likewise, in visual design, Gestalt helps us perceive the overall message of the design. If the design elements are arranged properly, the Gestalt of the overall design will be very clear.

Seeing the figure from the ground

As mentioned earlier, in the world of graphic design, space is often referred to as white space or negative space, especially in document design. In Gestalt theory, you can think of white space as something called "ground," basically the background of the slides. Elements we put on top are known as the "figure" in Gestalt. The Gestalt principle of "figure/ground" suggests that, because we have limited capacity for perceiving many elements at the same time, we naturally tend to visually simplify our world by focusing on one thing

Clear figure/ground relationships are very apparent in highway road signs, where it's important that viewers grasp the critical point(s) in an instant.

at a time. As we scan images, we unconsciously differentiate between ground (what's in the back) and figures (elements in front). This is one way we make sense of the world. As presenters, our job is to make it easier for viewers to get the most important points by making them pop out from the less important points. For the most part, the key elements we want to communicate are the figure elements; less important objects are ground.

Sometimes an element that is clearly figure (foreground) in one part of a slide becomes background (ground) as the eyes shift to a different part of the slide. This kind of tension—if created intentionally—adds a dynamic feel to a slide and keeps the viewer engaged. If you use a dynamic image in a slide along with text, in many cases the image is noticed first, and in this sense it feels more like figure. But the eye quickly turns to the text elements—your main message—that sit atop the image. Now the text is figure and the image is ground. Sometimes, it is a good idea to decrease the salience of the image by reducing the opacity or adding a blurring effect to make the figure/ground distinction more evident.

In this slide with a bulleted list, we will notice the background image first (in this sense it becomes figure), but we are quickly taken into the type, which now becomes figure. The type is clearly sitting on or in front of the image, but our eye may go from the type to the subject of the image and back again. This kind of figure-ground dynamic makes even simple visuals more interesting.

The slide contains a relevant and beautiful image, and the text is easy to read. There is nothing wrong with it, but if the background image had a blur effect the type would pop.

The photo used in this slide has a shallow depth of field that makes the image of the runner blurry. This effect serves to make the text pop more on the slide.

Directing the eyes

The Gestalt principle of "continuation" suggests techniques for helping the viewer's eyes flow smoothly—or continue—through a design from one object to another. The continuation effect is generally quite subtle, but it can be more obvious. For example, an obvious line of continuation is an arrow pointing to another element. You can achieve a more subtle form of continuation by aligning an important element with the line of sight of a human subject in a composition.

You'll notice the woman first, but your eyes are guided in an instant up to the type. (Images in slides from iStockphoto.com.)

The light is pointed in the direction of the type and literally shines a spotlight on the key message.

Children run toward the quotation (not away from it).

How can you not look at the type?

Using closure to engage viewers

Closure is another Gestalt principle that relates to how humans naturally tend to organize visual stimuli. The principle of closure says that a viewer's mind seeks completion. We will fill in—or close—gaps when necessary to make sense of a visual. The designer can use the viewer's natural tendency toward closure in many ways with the goal of bringing the viewer into the design and encouraging participation. For example, in traditional Japanese brush painting, a common object is the enso, or "circle of enlightenment." The incomplete circle is more dynamic and more engaging. It asks the viewer to visually complete the circle, which we naturally do without any confusion. Our brains fill in the gaps. When we use a part to imply a much bigger whole, the viewer becomes more involved in the visual.

The closure effect is not fully utilized as the tiger does not bleed off the edge of the slide.

Here, the slide feels bigger and we "see" the whole tiger, which is too big to fit on the screen.

Appreciating the subtle power of implied space

Recently, I saw a performance of Cirque du Soleil in Osaka. As always, it was an amazing show. The performance area was relatively small, but it felt much bigger during the show. Sounds that were part of the show were generated off stage, and performers often went into or came from the audience. The stage felt larger because the actions of the performers and set designers implied that it was larger.

In a similar way, we can create visual interest in a slide by "hiding" part of an object off the edge. This implies that something is happening "off stage." The implied space is the area outside what the viewer can see, creating an interesting visual tension. Implied space also takes advantage of the closure principle, our natural tendency to complete or close images.

Which slide creates more visual interest?

Implying depth

In addition to implying space to the audience, we can imply depth as well. For the most part, we create visuals that sit or display on a flat surface. To create a sense of depth, we can apply layering techniques, adjust the relative scale of objects, and use contrast and color to bring people in or out of the visual. The slide with the frogs here uses scale to create depth. The title slide with the photograph of the *wagasa* uses layers (and shadows) to imply a sense of depth.

Images in slides from iStockphoto.com.

Showing Restraint and Preserving Space

One reason the effective use of empty space is so rare in slide designs is that software companies keep throwing more and more features into their slideware. This tends to lead novice designers astray as they discover new ways to decorate and embellish. I don't really blame the software companies. They are, after all, in the business of satisfying customers by promising more value in costly updates, and some of the new features can be useful. Having many choices is generally a good thing, but it's up to us to exercise restraint.

Learn to love constraints

Our professional lives have become complicated by more and more choices, features, and options. But we know through experience that no freedom is to be found purely in the maximization of choices. In *The Paradox of Choice* (Ecco, 2003), author Barry Schwartz makes a similar claim. He says that having an unlimited array of choices and few constraints is not liberating or enabling—it is, instead, a burden and even bondage.

Schwartz, speaking from the consumer's point of view, believes that, in many cases, the abundance of choice does not make us more productive or improve our decisions. At the end of the book, Schwartz lists 11 ways we can halt the crippling effects of too much choice—"the tyranny of small decisions." The last item is simply this: "Learn to love constraints."

In *Buddhism Plain and Simple* (Broadway, 1998), Steve Hagen says that "...no freedom lies in maximizing petty choices." We all know this, but still we battle with the unnecessary and the nonessential. No one likes the idea of restrictions or fewer choices. But too many choices, options, features, and functions can become bondage that leads to poor decision making—such as adding more when removing more and exercising restraint is a better option.

True freedom doesn't lie in the maximization of choice, but, ironically, is most easily found in a life where there is little choice.
— Steve Hagen

When more is less

When embarking on a presentation, the most frightening thing for many people is the empty slide—a blank slate without even a template (gasp!). So, under pressure and the common belief that "no one ever got fired for including too much data in a deck of PowerPoint slides," the novice designer adds more and more just to be safe. Unfortunately, too many elements placed without thoughtful consideration of what to include and what to exclude often leads to wasted space and clutter.

What does it *feel like* to be confronted with too many options? To view designs made without adequate use of constraints? I found a good description of how this kind of complication feels in *Learning to See Creatively* by Bryan Peterson (Amphoto Books, 2003). Peterson talks about how inexperienced photographers often snap photos that have too many points of interest—too many elements that alienate the eyes, causing them to move on. This lack of direction in the composition fails to engage or satisfy viewers, so they look elsewhere. Viewers are left feeling a bit of confusion that Peterson describes like this:

> *Imagine finding yourself lost on the open road. You finally see a lone gas station up ahead, you're hungry to discover the route back to the freeway. You ask the attendant for directions, and he begins to offer plan A and plan B and plan C, each with varying degrees of specific detail. Rather than finding the clear, simple, and concise directions you were seeking, your brain is now swimming in a sea of even greater confusion. Clear, simple, and concise directions are all that you wanted.*

We've all had a similar feeling while exploring a poorly designed Web site, using a nonintuitive software application, or gazing at a confusing and cluttered deck of slides. Learning to first see white space may be the first step toward designing effective visuals. But restraint concerning what you add to that space is the second step. Learning to see—and then learning to preserve—space gives your visual messages more impact and greater clarity.

Exercise: Less-Is-More Group Slide Activity

When I conduct day-long private training sessions at corporations around the world, we do a group activity in the afternoon to get everyone involved. I ask a few presenters from the firm (salespeople, researchers, executives, etc.) to take us through the visuals used in an important talk. They do not present—they simply show each slide onscreen, explain the purpose of the slide, and attempt to justify the visual in terms of its effectiveness in a live talk. The group then attempts to answer two simple questions:

1. Can we eliminate the slide?
2. If the slide is essential, what can we remove to make it more effective?

After spending the morning looking at design concepts and rethinking their entire approach to presentations, the group is eager to critique their own slides and the slides created by others. Sometimes, the clutter and the superfluous elements are so obvious that the slides evoke laughter from both the presenter charged with defending the older design and the team members assigned with critiquing the design. Because we are using actual slide decks from the participants, this critiquing exercise is very effective for generating concrete recommendations for immediate use.

You can try this activity with your own group. Look for a presentation deck in your organization that is typical of the kind used for live talks. As a group, sit down together in a nonthreatening environment and go through each slide. Determine what the purpose of the visual is and how careful reduction of elements can improve the visual's ability to achieve its purpose.

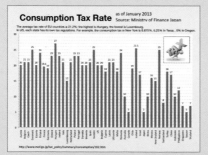

The purpose of this slide is to compare Japan's consumption tax rate with other countries, but is that difference easy to see at a glance?

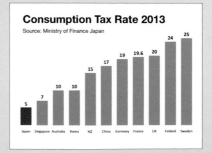

Here, you can see the difference at a glace. What design elements were removed and what changes were made to make it easier to see?

In Sum

- White space allows for real differences to be created, emphasized, and noticed. The space allows for elements such as text, images, and lines to breathe. Just like life itself, it is this invisible breath that sustains and empowers.

- Balance among parts contributes to harmony and keeps viewers engaged. A balance among elements helps activate negative space and smoothly guide the viewer's eyes from one part of the design to another.

- Adding space to your designs makes it easier for the audience to understand the most important points of your presentation. Significant points should pop out more than less important points. You can also use implied space and depth in your designs to create an interesting visual tension.

- Learning to first *see* white space is the first step toward designing effective visuals; restraint concerning what you add to that space is the second step.

8

Creating Purpose and Focus

When we look at a presentation screen, we look for patterns, differences, and similarities to interpret the speaker's meaning. We do this naturally, without ever really thinking about it. Why is this? Perhaps this is just how our species evolved. There certainly seems to have been an evolutionary advantage for those who were skilled at noticing danger, spotting food, and locating a mate. Seeing differences, and being able to quickly act on them, was as important for survival in our evolutionary history as it is today. We are visual beings and taking note of contrast and affinity—that is, differences and similarities—plays a large role in how we make sense of the world.

The typical bullet point–filled slide fails to take advantage of an audience's great capacity to understand visuals while also listening to a presenter's words. People cannot read loads of text and listen to someone speak at the same time. They can, however, listen to a presenter and look at quantitative and supportive visuals. In this way, the visual amplifies the narration.

Many ineffective slides can be improved by simply making it clear to the viewer what is important and what is less important. Guiding viewers with purposeful choices in the design and leading the viewers' eyes with clear focal points in a slide presentation takes better advantage of the audience members' natural ability to process visual information quickly.

Differences Provide Context and Meaning

We naturally pay attention to—and in many cases are stimulated by—things that change due to differences created. Change is essential to life and to good stories, art, and design. In music, for example, you'll find that in just one song, numerous changes may occur that engage you and take you on a journey. Sometimes the music can be fast and lively (allegro), and at other times slower (adagio). Sometimes the notes are short and detached from each other (staccato), and at other times the notes are played more smoothly (legato). And a single piece of music may have key changes, time-signature changes, and so on. When these differences occur in the music, a story is unfolding in much the same way that a well-designed presentation unfolds.

The art of storytelling

Life is about conflict and resolution, about problems and obstacles, and then overcoming those problems. In the real world, if you have no contrast or no change—if there are no "highs" or "lows"—you have about the dullest life imaginable. Likewise, in design, if everything is the same, then where is the story in that? Unless your intention is to produce a presentation that goes unnoticed, creating changes and clear differences is essential.

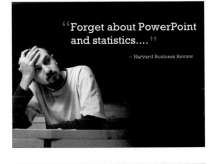

Yet similarity is important, too. If everything is different, then contrast is weakened. If everything is important, then nothing is important. If everything stands out, then nothing stands out. As with all things, balance must be maintained. People may be naturally inclined to scan and look for contrast, patterns, and meaning—but they will give up pretty quickly if our designs confuse the eye. Our job is to know what the key points are and to create the differences that makes it easy for viewers to naturally discover them. Remember, the design gives our stories focus and order.

Images in slides from iStockphoto.com.

What does story have to do with change and contrast? At its core, story is about a "...fundamental conflict between subjective expectation and cruel reality," says legendary screenwriter Robert McKee. Story is about imbalance and opposing forces, or about a problem that must be worked out. A good storyteller describes what it's like to deal with these opposing forces "...calling on the protagonist to dig deeper, work with scarce resources, make difficult decisions...and ultimately discover the truth," says McKee.

Why can't a presentation on a technical or scientific topic be a story about a long journey of discovery, of trial and error, and so on? (A story with plenty of data and information presented along the way, of course.) Creating change and contrasts is fundamental to good storytelling, and this goes for visual storytelling as well.

Perceiving differences in nature

If you really pay attention, you'll see that our visual world is full of contrasts. This black-and-white photograph is a wonderful example of the contrasting elements we can see in nature. In this composition of Mt. Fuji, you can see that the hills and mountains in the foreground are darker and the mountains get progressively lighter in the distance. This gradient from dark to light is something artists and designers use to add depth to their compositions.

When you looked at this image for the first time, you probably noticed Mt. Fuji first. Although it is a lighter shade, it is also much larger and higher than the other elements. As you notice the dark gray foreground elements, your eye is naturally taken back to the base and then up Mt. Fuji.

The lesson here is that size and value (lightness and darkness) can be used to achieve depth or create a feeling of perspective. On a light background, darker items appear as foreground elements. When elements have less contrast and get lighter, they recede and appear farther away. On a dark background, the lighter elements will have higher contrast, and it is the darker elements that appear to recede as they approach a tonal quality closer to the background color.

Presenting with variety and depth

As mentioned earlier when discussing text, color, images, and graphs, there are endless ways to combine the elements in a design. Not only that, elements can vary in terms of size, location, color, value, texture, shape, position, alignment, implied movement, and on and on. The only real limitation is your own imagination. The key point, however, is to be aware of your intention and use the elements in a way that gets your point across the best. Below are a few sample slides that illustrate contrast using only simple shapes and changes.

Contrast in size.

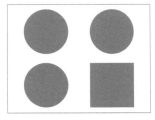

Contrast in shape.

Contrast in orientation.

Contrast in position.

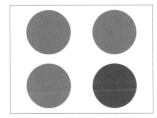

Contrast in tone (value).

Contrast in hue (color).

Contrast elements with purpose

Most people place elements without devoting much thought to which will be noticed first, second, and so on. It's important to think about what messages you want the audience to understand loud and clear and then to make those points by adding contrast to your elements and establishing meaning. Contrast can be very obvious and it can be more subtle, but it should never be confusing or weak.

Large foreground elements can create depth

Hiroshige, a popular Japanese artist of the Edo period, was known for his colorful wood block prints, including a series called *One Hundred Famous Views of Edo*. In some of his compositions, Hiroshige brought in large foreground elements that were cut off as they extended far outside the frame. You can see this in the large, drooping branches in the *Yatsumi no hashi* composition pictured here.

Introducing such a large foreground element establishes depth by creating a big difference in size between the foreground, middle ground, and background elements. We can apply something similar to elements in slides, too.

Images in slides from iStockphoto.com.

Tokonoma and the Art of the Focal Point

iStockphoto.com

Every good design needs a focal point—including interior living spaces. In many Western homes, the mantelpiece in the living room is a focal point from which other interior design elements are added in a more or less symmetrical fashion. In traditional Japanese homes or modern homes containing a *washitsu* (Japanese-style room), the *tokonoma* (床の間) serves as the subtle focal point for the interior. The tokonoma (floor/bed + space) is a raised alcove in which Japanese art such as a *kakemono* (hanging scroll) or a flower arrangement is displayed.

The custom of having this built-in recessed space in a Japanese room goes back more than 500 years. While the tokonoma has lost much of its early religious nature, it's still very much an honored part of the Japanese room. Standing inside the tokonoma is not allowed. When you gather in a traditional Japanese room, the most honored guest is seated in front of the tokonoma. However, in another example of traditional Japanese refinement and humility, the guest is traditionally seated facing away from the tokonoma, so the homeowner does not appear to be showing off the artistic content of the tokonoma. In the West, the mantel often has a large picture or other artifact hanging above it that remains for years. By contrast, the artwork in the tokonoma changes throughout the year based on the season or the occasion.

Historically, the Japanese people did not use furniture; they sat on warm and comfortable *tatami* mats. Therefore, washitsu rooms felt spacious regardless of size—there was virtually nothing else in the room to distract your attention. The emptiness or exclusion of nonessential decoration allows even the smallest rooms to feel more spacious and guides the eyes to the focal point of the room.

Because the room is not cluttered with myriad furnishings, souvenirs, and other possessions, it is easier to notice and then linger on the art contained in the tokonoma.

A bare washitsu, built with natural elements, is a design with a close connection to nature. This harmonious balance with nature, and the garden just outside the walls of the room, is reflected in the seasonal contents of the tokonoma itself. In a way, the spaciousness of the room extends beyond the room to the vastness of the outside world.

You can also learn about focal points through *chashitsu* (traditional-style tearooms), which come in many sizes (but are typically 4.5 tatami mats in size). The materials to build the tearoom (or a tea house) are simple and rustic in the *wabi* (simple, fresh, clean) style. The tokonoma in a Japanese tearoom is carefully situated to be the focal point of the room. In most cases, you enter the tearoom directly across from the tokonoma, so the artistic content is the first thing in the room you notice. As Okakura Kakuzo notes in *The Book of Tea* (Dover, 1964), as guests quietly enter the tearoom, they first make "obeisance to the picture or flower arrangement on the tokonoma." The walls of a chashitsu, and the traditional Japanese-style rooms in general, are kept bare and simple.

Lessons from the tokonoma

You can apply the following lessons from the tokonoma to presentation design and other forms of design:

- A powerful focal point need not be overbearing or fancy.

- Emptiness creates spaciousness that assists the viewer in discovering the focal point.

- Subtle contrasts consisting of fewer elements create interest.

- Excluding the decorative and nonessential from other areas allows a focal point to be created using only simple elements (or a single element).

- If you intentionally create an area of contrast, it brings the viewer into the primary focal point and guides their eyes to the secondary focal point, the third, and so on without confusion.

- Eschew symmetry in favor of asymmetrical balance where possible.

Establishing a Strong Design Priority

For years I have asked designers in Japan what they believe to be the most common causes of poor, ineffective designs. One of the most common answers is the problem of a weak design priority. Design priority, another way of saying focal point, is based on a determined assignment of value or importance to different elements.

When a viewer sees a design for the first time—a slide, poster, page, and so on—he or she is naturally and instantly attracted to whatever stands out. Problems arise for communication when (1) nothing really pops out, (2) too many things pop out, or (3) superfluous elements pop out unintentionally and become a distraction. Any of these problems can clutter the visual design and confuse the viewer.

The presenter must be consciously aware of what he or she wants the viewer to notice first, second, third, and so on. Nothing can be by accident. Visuals with a strong design priority often use contrast to get attention and guide the viewer's eye through a design.

Good slide designs have many things in common with good designs found in billboards and posters. What's important for a billboard to be effective? At the very least, a poster or billboard must (1) get noticed, (2) be understood, and (3) be remembered. Slides are a bit like this: We want the visual elements onscreen to get attention and draw the viewer in. Once drawn in by the element that pops out the most, the viewer is guided by design priority and the various contrasts among the elements to illuminate the points you are making. In the end, this hierarchy helps create messages that are more meaningful— messages that target the viewer's visual and verbal channel.

This sign in downtown Osaka, Japan, really pops out, mostly because of its unusual orientation.

Dominance and structure

Another way of looking at a design's effectiveness is in terms of dominance, which is related to design priority or focal point. Every good visual has a clearly dominant element that lets the viewer know where to begin.

The larger or more dominant elements are generally going to rank higher in the structure in most designs, but this is not always the case. For example, a very large type size used in a declarative sentence across the top of a slide would usually be highest in the ranking, but if a large photograph is used in the slide, the text may attract the eyes second.

Juxtapositions among the elements guide the viewer along invisible lines to other elements. Contrasts between light and dark, emptiness and content, and so on create interest and energy and help the viewer navigate without having to figure out what is important and what is subordinate.

In the first example (left) it's not clear where our eyes should go first. The type at the top is weak and every bar is a different color, emphasizing nothing. We may notice the photo first, but it leads us nowhere. The slides below do a better job of leading the eyes, have a clear hierarchy, and are easy to understand quickly. (Images in slides from iStockphoto.com.)

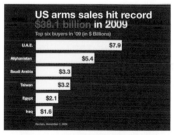

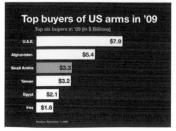

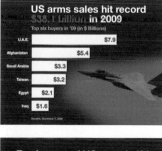

Low background salience

Salience is an important concept to consider when drawing attention to your message. According to Harvard professor Stephen Kosslyn, author of *Clear and to the Point* (Oxford University Press, 2007), understanding the principle of salience is one key to designing visuals that direct and hold attention. Salience suggests that "attention is drawn to large perceptible differences." The most important element of your design should also be the most salient, says Kosslyn.

You can do this in many ways, such as with larger or bold type, color choices, positioning, and myriad other techniques that help guide the viewer's eyes.

Generally, the slide backgrounds themselves should have relatively low salience. That is, backgrounds should be simple without lots of perceptible differences in the background image itself as this would interfere with the foreground elements. (And if you use a photo for a background image, use a photo that supports your message instead of undermining it. A good background, Kosslyn says, can "allow you to underline your message effectively, or it can create confusion. The background image should not conflict with the message of the display.")

Ambiguity between foreground and background elements often leads to weak visuals, confusion, and possibly even eyestrain. Backgrounds with patterns should be avoided as they have too much salience.

You can use images as backgrounds, but there must be clear contrast with the elements on top. The examples here show better contrast as you move from left to right. (Images in slides on this page and opposite page from iStockphoto.com.)

The preference for people

We are naturally drawn to images of people, and we're especially drawn to images of faces. We even have a tendency to see a face where a face does not actually exist, such as in an unusual pattern on the surface of a cheese sandwich or cinnamon bun or in a low-resolution photo of the surface of Mars. Images of people get our attention like few other images can.

The important thing to know is that if you use images of people—whether or not you intend for the image to be a focal point—you must know that this is where people are going to look first. If other elements are of greater importance, then make sure you place those elements so that the viewer's eye will naturally flow from the image to those elements.

In the first slide, you probably find yourself continually drawn to the woman's face, even though the speaker's key points appear in the upper-left corner. In the slide on the right, the image also gets your attention first, but it is easy for your eyes to flow off the image and up to the key point of the slide. The image is pointing in the direction of the data and we are not continually drawn to the image (unless you are really hungry, I suppose).

The first example above shows the face of the person who is being quoted, a leader in the company. You notice the face first, and her eye gaze takes you naturally to the text. In the next slide the image of the woman is not so strong, but still the eye gaze and general physical orientation of the person take you back to the text.

Simple slides that guide the eyes

Take a look at a few before-and-after slides. The "after" slides are the kind used in support of live talks where all of the words are coming from the speaker. The slides on the left show a rather arbitrary placement of elements and have poor hierarchy and dominance. While the slides at left have contrast, it is not clear why some things stand out and others do not. What are we supposed to look at first, second, third? The eye tends to wander.

The slides on the right have better design priority or focal point. First, removing extraneous information from the slides improves the clarity. The samples here are very simple, but you can apply the general idea to more complex slides as well. Just be clear in your own mind where you want people to go first when the visual is shown.

BEFORE ▼   AFTER ▼

Not only does the slide at left have too much text for a live talk, it's not clear where the eye is supposed to go first. We may notice the pictures, but they are very small. Usually, the text at the top is the most important, but why is it so weak? In the text on the right, our eyes go to the jogger and then quickly to the key point in the text.

BEFORE ▼   AFTER ▼

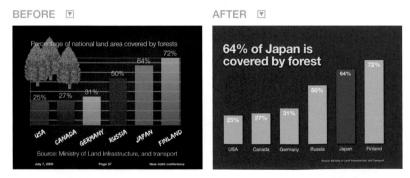

The slide at left has too many colors—our eyes bounce around from one colorful column to the next. What's the key point of the slide? Hard to tell. In the slide at right, our eyes go to the large text first and then the blue column (or vice versa) and then we look at the other columns.

BEFORE ▼   AFTER ▼

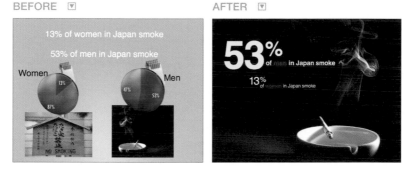

The key point is that a lot of Japanese men smoke—and more men than women smoke by a large margin. In the slide at left, it takes a while to figure that out. Our eyes roam from the pictures to the pie charts to the cigarettes and then to the light text. In the slide at right, the key point stands out. You may notice the photo first, but you are quickly moved up through the smoke to the large text, which is the key point.

BEFORE ▼   AFTER ▼

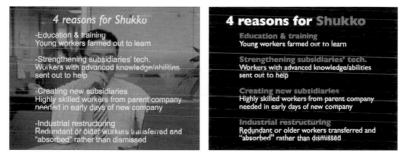

Sometimes, you may want to review key points or definitions by placing those definitions in text form in your slide. The background image in the slide at left has too much salience. The contrast with the text is weak and the information is very hard to read. It's difficult to tell what is the subhead and what is the definition because the text is the same weight. The slide at right is very easy to scan from top to bottom.

Images in slides from iStockphoto.com.

Adding Motion to Make a Point

When you look at a slide, the first thing you probably notice is the element with the largest size or most vivid color. The elements we cannot ignore, however, are the elements that move. We humans—and virtually all other animals—are wired to notice movement above all else. Because we are so quick to notice it, designers must use animation and transitions with great reserve.

There is no reason to animate every item that appears on a slide. You add motion to your slides essentially for these reasons: (1) to emphasize part of a visual, (2) to draw attention to a single element, (3) to bring in elements as you build your point visually, or (4) to create a change to propel your point forward. Simple graphs like most of those shown in this book do not need to be animated. Yet, more complex charts or diagrams may be more easily understood if you can build the components in a step-by-step fashion.

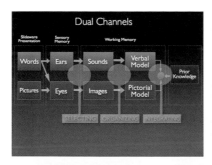

I used this slide years ago to explain (in Japanese) the Dual Channels of cognition as explained in Richard Mayer's *Multimedia Learning* (Cambridge University Press, 2001). Components faded in from left to right as I explained the process. Below is the Japanese version of the slides showing the progression. This is not overly complex information, but the idea is easier to understand if the presenter takes the time to build the components slowly while speaking, adding examples along the way.

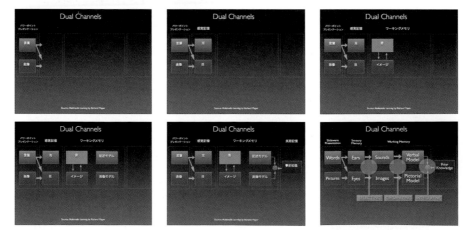

Using subtle transitions to show change

To present statistics on labor issues in Japan, I first show images of farmers and then highlight their challenges. The first slide shows a woman planting rice. This image dissolves to a version of the same photo with a Gaussian blur effect applied to add depth and make the type and simple line chart stand out more from the photo, which has now become the background. The colored text boxes are a darker shade of the blue from the field. The lines in the graph are imperfect for a more organic "earthy" feel. (Images in slides from iStockphoto.com.)

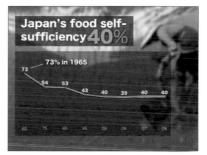

Here, I am discussing the low fertility rate in Japan. I begin with a photo I took of children at one of the fall festivals near my home in Nara. As I ask the question concerning the current fertility rate, the photo dissolves to a blurred version of the same image, which pushes the image back and makes the type pop out more. Finally, the answer and the line chart fade in to reveal the trend. The yellow used for the line and highlighted type matches the yellow in the background.

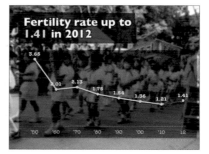

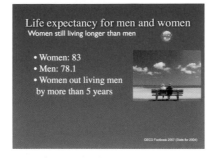

The original slide, about life expectancy in Australia, was a rather typical, static slide. How could you show the difference in life expectancy in a more emotional way? One way is to take one slide and break it up into four slides that subtly animate via smooth dissolves (transitions) to tell a story. It is impossible to replicate the emotional effect of these animated slides in a book, but the four slides below should give you an idea.

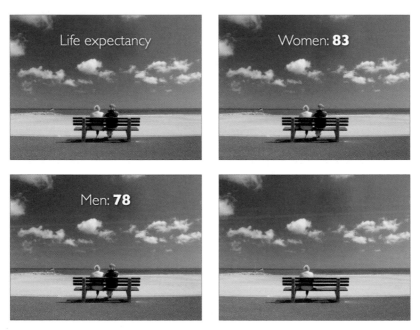

You can add a transition (dissolve) to smoothly change the text in sync with the narration. As the last slide dissolves in, it appears that the man fades out from the scene, creating a very emotional statement. (Image in slides from iStockphoto.com.)

In Sum

- People are naturally inclined to scan and look for contrast, patterns, and meaning. Our job as presenters is to know what the key points are and create the differences that make it easy for the viewer to naturally discover these points. Meaningful contrasts give our stories focus and order.

- Slides are similar to posters or billboards in that they must (1) get noticed, (2) be understood, and (3) be remembered. The visual elements onscreen serve to get attention and draw the viewer in. Once drawn into the element that pops out the most, the viewer is guided by design priority and various contrasts among the elements to an understanding of the points you are trying to make.

- Every good visual has a clearly dominant element that attracts attention and lets the viewer know where to begin. The presenter must be consciously aware of what he or she wants the viewer to notice first, second, third, and so on. Viewers tend to focus on images of people first. If you're using images of people, make sure this is where you want the eye to go first.

- Add movement to your slides to emphasize part of a visual or draw attention to a single element. Bring in elements as you build your point visually and create a change to propel your point forward.

9

Achieving Harmony

Every individual slide and every slide deck should feel like it is part of a unified whole. When you have unity, the elements are congruous, creating a general perception that things are connected and part of the same message. As we observed in Chapter 7, your slides should elicit a feeling of "this design works," when looking at the whole.

It's true that we also want variety within individual slides and across the series of slides used in the presentation. Depending on the audience and topic, the variety may even be quite dramatic. However, we still need a clear sense that the elements are somehow part of the same message and part of the larger whole. When elements are not connected on some level, if they seem not to fit together or feel unrelated, then we have a disharmonious design and communication suffers.

The separate elements that comprise a design are important, but on top of that, if you achieve unity, then the whole of the design seems larger than the sum of the individual parts. If the viewer sees only a potpourri of objects and parts— even though they may be interesting parts—then visual unity is not achieved.

The photo to the left is an example of traditional Japanese architecture. The Japanese aesthetic does not deny nature but attempts to bring it into the abode in a way that is harmonious. Yes, presentation slides are not the same thing as a traditional Japanese home or tea house, but to the degree they can, our design elements must also work together in harmony.

Simplify to Unify

The world is full of too much visual stimuli for anyone to handle without attempting to simplify it. That's why we naturally look for patterns and order in our visual environment. Viewers naturally seek out organization and unity.

You can achieve unity in visuals with many elements. It's even easier to achieve unity, however, with fewer elements. Simplicity doesn't always mean working toward minimalism, but a thoughtful reduction of nonessential items is a good first step toward arranging elements that reflect both unity and variety. Uncluttered visuals with fewer elements allow viewers to easily see the harmonious relationships among the unifying elements. If the visuals consist of too many objects or too great a variety among objects, your slides will look incongruous.

A common error that presentation designers make is throwing together too many color schemes, fonts, and graphs that contain too many style variations. Notice the differences in each series of four slides below. The content is the same, yet the bottom row of slides looks more unified and is easier to understand in an instant.

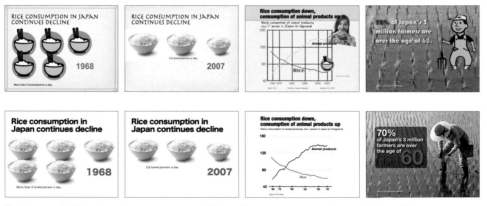

The top row of slides shown here uses too many different fonts, colors, and backgrounds along with a mix of clip art and photographs. Almost no elements are repeated. In the bottom row of slides, high-quality photographs and a single highlight color are used for a clean, harmonious look. The slides clearly look like they belong together. (Images in slides from iStockphoto.com.)

Noticing the Similarities

Another way to achieve harmony across a deck of slides is to use similar elements. For example, you'll give your design a solid sense of agreement if you use high-quality, black-and-white photography throughout rather than a mix of cheap clip art, black-and-white photos, and common color stock images. Or, you can use similar items conceptually in your design, such as things found in Japan. For a slide presentation, an interesting background theme used consistently throughout the entire presentation adds visual unity. Objects can be similar (or dissimilar) in many respects, such as in shape, color, and size.

What is it about these four slides that unifies them and makes them feel part of a whole?

When choosing typefaces, think in terms of finding a similar, harmonious feel that matches the theme of the content. If you have a radical, edgy presentation with edgy, dramatic photography, perhaps a typeface with an unusual and radical feel will give harmony and unity to your message (as long as it's legible).

BEFORE ▼   AFTER ▼

The typefaces used in the slides in the left column are not only hard to read, they do not match the tone of the content. The slides in the right column use type that is more harmonious with the content of the message. (Images in slides from iStockphoto.com.)

Providing Visual Cues

To help the audience follow your story, you can offer clear visual cues or sign-posts, or even provide an audio signal for getting your audience's attention. You might use a recurring element or theme as a way to achieve some rhythm—such as a certain typeface, a poignant line, a recurring shape, a color, a particular use of space, and so on. It will tie your story together and provide unity to the composition if you provide meaningful cues throughout.

You can use a recurring image to signal to the audience where you are in the story. Here, I introduce the six key aptitudes outlined in Dan Pink's best-selling book *A Whole New Mind* (Riverhead Trade, 2006) in one of the first slides in the presentation. Although I use many slides in between, at the start of each section the original six-aptitudes slide reappears with only the current topic highlighted to remind the audience where we are in the journey.

You need unity so that your message comes out clear and strong, but you also need variety in the design to add interest and grab attention. If the design has too much variety, however, then even if certain items are repeated with an eye toward creating a unified feel, the repetition effect will be lost in a sea of clutter. You have heard me say it before, but in all things there must be balance.

Images in slides from iStockphoto.com.

Connecting the Elements

You can give visuals a unified, harmonious feel by making sure that all the elements on a slide are visually connected to each other. Sometimes, this means connecting many elements via an invisible or implied line. At other times, a particular element may align with just one other element. You do not have to connect every element with something else in the slide, but if an element is unconnected, the effect should be intentional and for a good reason.

The disharmony produced by a poor connection of elements gives visuals an unprofessional feel that impairs the natural flow of the eye through a design. Using even a very simple grid (discussed later in this chapter) for your slide elements' arrangement makes aligning objects easier and produces a more connected design.

Revisiting Gestalt theory, the law of proximity says that "spatial or temporal proximity of elements may induce the mind to perceive a collective or totality." In other words, people have a natural tendency to assume that elements that are physically close to each other are related, and elements that are further apart are not. You can achieve greater harmony and help your viewers understand your visuals by making sure related items are clearly positioned close to each other. Grouping elements, then, allows the viewer to simplify things based on their location. The closer the items are, the more likely they are to be seen as related or together.

BEFORE ▼   AFTER ▼

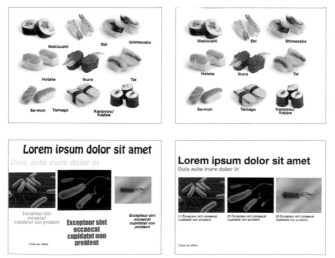

The slides in the right column do a much better job of connecting the elements. It must always be clear what belongs together and what does not. For example, it should be very easy to tell which image the type is meant to align with in a design. (Images in slides from iStockphoto.com.)

Using a Grid to Provide Structure

A grid provides an invisible structure for placing and connecting elements to produce better clarity and connectedness. When a grid works well, elements within a design feel like they are part of a whole—that they belong together. Using a grid helps us build a clear, simple hierarchy among elements.

Using a grid, however, does not mean that the design becomes rigid or boring. You still have the freedom to be creative and original within the arrangement. Sometimes, the greatest source of creative solutions comes only when we have a structure within which to work. Jazz, for example, may seem like a free-for-all of creative expression without boundaries to those who are unfamiliar with it. In fact, there are rules and structure and boundaries that are "invisible" to the listener, but provide a liberating kind of "grid" for the musicians to communicate and express themselves. The end result is that the whole (the music) is greater than the sum of the notes played by the individual players.

Using a grid in presentation design is a bit like this. It's the simple grid underneath—and implied on top—that gives us greater ease of arrangement and ultimately more freedom to experiment with the elements that comprise our messages. The unity that is created makes for clear, harmonious designs.

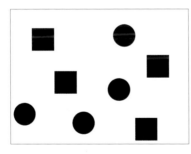

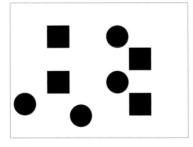

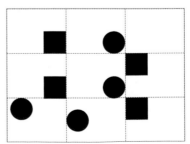

The simple shapes in the first slide above look random and appear to have no organization or connection to each other. In the second slide above, the shapes seem at least a bit more connected somehow, even if we do not detect a clear pattern. By moving the shapes just slightly so that they are connected via a simple 3x3 grid, a more harmonious effect is created.

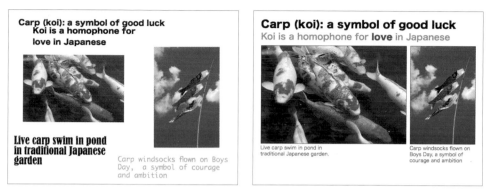

The first slide is a mess as none of the elements align with each other. I used a grid to resize and align elements to fit together in a more unified way. If you have many elements that must be aligned, a more complex grid like the one I used here may work well. Usually, however, a much simpler grid is all you need to help you unify elements on a slide. (Images in slides from iStockphoto.com.)

A few notes about grids

- A grid consists of both vertical and horizontal lines that are spread out at even distances and intersect, forming an underlying network or skeleton to build on.

- You can create an intricate and detailed grid or you can use one that is very, very simple. The grid you need depends on your intentions, but generally even a very simple grid makes it easier to unify elements on a slide or any other "canvas" you may be using.

- You can create any kind of grid using the guides and grids built into your software.

- Personally, I find a five-column/four-row (5 x 4) grid to be both simple and flexible for many situations. Yet the grid I use the most—my default grid— is the simple rule of thirds.

In this slide from a presentation on the history of the wagasa in Japan, the photos and type are arranged using a six-column/four-row (6 x 4) grid.

Here are the same elements using a five-column/four-row (5 x 4) grid.

Rule of thirds

One of the easiest grids to use is a 3 x 3 grid that utilizes the "rule of thirds." This rule is a compositional technique that is one of the first lessons visual artists and designers learn early in their education. Photographers have been using the rule of thirds for years as well.

According to the rule of thirds, images may appear more interesting, engaging, dynamic, and compelling if the subject is not placed in the center. (This also applies to video scenes.) Of course, dead center is where beginning photographers and novice videographers tend to put their subjects, because it seems the best way to emphasize them. If you try moving your subject away from the center, however, nearer to a "power point" (where the gridlines intersect), you can create a more powerful or interesting visual by creating a bit of tension or even drama.

Using the rule of thirds to guide your designs is a simple thing, and it's one of the very basic things the pros do so well. Everyone can design better slides—and take better snapshots and shoot better video—by keeping the rule of thirds in mind. (Note, however, that it's more of a compositional guideline than a rule, and it's no panacea for poor design.) You will find that you can apply the rule of thirds to presentation visuals to give them a more balanced and professional look. Below are some sample slides created over a simple 3 x 3 grid.

I built these slides for various presentations on top of a simple 3 x 3, or "rule of thirds," grid. (Images in slides from iStockphoto.com.)

I built these slides with a 3 x 3 grid as well. Can you envision the grid sitting under these slides? (Images in slides from iStockphoto.com.)

Harmony and the bento

A Japanese *bento* is an elegant box that contains a kind of *washoku* (Japanese food). Remember that *wa,* which designates something Japanese-made or in a Japanese style, literally means harmony. This is appropriate because traditional Japanese meals—including the humble bento—are prepared and arranged in a harmonious, unified manner. The bento box itself is a type of grid in addition to being a container.

When preparing the bento, the chef considers the types of flavors that go well together in one meal. Foods are also chosen in terms of color and texture to create a pleasing, subtle unified appeal. Sometimes, the ingredients and the theme match the season.

Recently, I took this photo with my iPhone on the Shinkansen (bullet train). In this meal of relatively modest calories and high nutrition, an amazing 20 different varieties of food are contained within the small box. It all fits together harmoniously in spite of the complexity of putting so many elements into such a small area. The shape of the "grid" contained within the bento box makes this possible.

Emptiness is the foundation of infinite possibilities.

— Daisetsu T. Suzuki,
author and scholar

10 Japanese Aesthetic Principles to Consider

Exposing ourselves to traditional Japanese aesthetic ideas—notions that may seem foreign to many of us—is a good exercise in *lateral thinking*, a term coined by Edward de Bono in 1967. "Lateral thinking is for changing concepts and perception," says de Bono. Thinking about harmony in design by exploring the tenets of the Zen aesthetic may not be an example of lateral thinking in the strict sense, but doing so is a good exercise in stretching our minds and really beginning to think differently about visuals and design in our everyday professional lives.

The Zen aesthetic principles found in the art of the traditional Japanese garden, for example, have many lessons for us, though they are unknown to most people. The principles are interconnected and overlapping; it's not possible to simply put the ideas in separate boxes. Thankfully, Patrick Lennox Tierney, a recipient of the Order of the Rising Sun in 2007 in Japan, wrote a few short essays elaborating on the following concepts. This list covers only ten of the design-related principles that govern the aesthetics of the Japanese garden and other art forms in Japan. Perhaps they will stimulate your creativity and get you thinking in a new way about your own design challenges.

1. **Kanso** (簡素)**:** Simplicity or elimination of clutter. Things are expressed in a plain, simple, natural manner. Kanso reminds us to think not in terms of decoration, but in terms of clarity—a kind of clarity that may be achieved through omission or exclusion of the nonessential.

2. **Fukinsei** (不均整)**:** Asymmetry or irregularity. The idea of controlling balance in a composition via irregularity and asymmetry is a central tenet of the Zen aesthetic. The *enso* (Zen circle) in brush painting, for example, is often drawn as an incomplete circle, symbolizing the imperfection that is part of existence. In graphic design, too, asymmetrical balance is a dynamic, beautiful thing. Try looking for or creating beauty in balanced asymmetry. Nature itself is full of beautiful and harmonious relationships that are asymmetrical yet balanced. This is a dynamic beauty that attracts and engages.

3. **Shibui/Shibumi** (渋味)**:** Beautiful by being understated, or by being precisely what it is meant to be and not elaborated upon. Direct and simple, without being flashy. Elegant simplicity, articulate brevity. The term is sometimes used today to describe something cool but beautifully minimalist, including technology and some consumer products. (Shibui literally means bitter tasting.)

4. **Shizen** (自然)**:** Naturalness. Absence of pretense or artificiality, full creative intent unforced. Ironically, the spontaneous nature of the Japanese garden the viewer perceives is not accidental. This is a reminder that design is not an accident, even when we are trying to create a natural-feeling environment. It is not raw nature as such, but one with more purpose and intention.

5. **Yūgen** (幽玄)**:** Profundity or suggestion rather than revelation. A Japanese garden, for example, can be described as a collection of subtleties and symbolic elements. Photographers and designers can surely think of many ways to visually imply more by not showing the whole—that is, showing more by showing less.

6. **Datsuzoku** (脱俗)**:** Freedom from habit or formula. Escape from the daily routine or the ordinary. Unworldly. Transcending the conventional. This principle describes the feeling of surprise and a bit of amazement when people realize they can have freedom from the conventional. Professor Tierney says that the Japanese garden itself, "…made with the raw materials of nature and its success in revealing the essence of natural things to us is an ultimate surprise. Many surprises await at almost every turn in a Japanese Garden."

7. **Seijaku** (静寂)**:** Tranquility or an energized calm (quiet), stillness, solitude. This is related to the feeling you may have when in a Japanese garden. The opposite feeling to one expressed by seijaku is noise and disturbance. How might we bring a feeling of "active calm" and stillness to ephemeral designs outside the Zen arts?

8. **Wa** (和)**:** Harmony, peace, balance. Wa is the character that designates something as Japanese or Japanese-made such as in *washoku* (food), *washitsu* (room style), *wafuku* (traditional clothes), *wagasa* (traditional umbrella), and so on. The idea of harmony and balance is fundamental to Japanese culture and human relationships. Harmony is a key aspect of design sensibilities in Japan. Aesthetically, wa is fundamental to all good design.

9. **Ma** (間)**:** Empty, spatial void, interval of space or time. The concept of ma can be found in many of the Zen arts, including traditional gardens and ikebana, Noh theater, and so on. Ma does not just mean the kind of empty space that is background; the emptiness is often arranged to be a focal point. Ma allows for an energy or sense of movement within a design. Ma may show itself in traditional music in the form of silence or pauses. In ikebana the idea of emptiness allows for each flower to breathe and also reveals the contrasts and the balance found in the asymmetrical arrangement.

10. **Yohaku-no-bi** (余白の美)**:** Appreciation of the beauty found in that portion that is implied, unstated, or unexpressed in a work of art. An idea close to the modern idea of "less is more." Its focus is on what was left out. Related to the Zen ideal of ku (emptiness) and mu (nothingness). You can see the ideal expressed in Zen gardens that feature large sections of raked sand or gravel and in ink paintings that leave large sections of the paper untouched. The term literally means "beauty of extra white." Although the term dates back centuries, you still hear it today.

Harmony Checklist

As discussed, you have many options for creating harmony in your slides. Ask the following questions after looking at your own presentation slides to determine if your slides contain harmony and unity:

- Is there a clear hierarchy?
- Are there clear signposts for viewers to follow?
- Is there a clear focal point?
- Have you used some contrast in your elements to emphasize the focal point?
- Are the elements professional looking and well aligned?
- Is type formatted with only one or two typeface families?
- Are related items clearly related?
- Do photos or other visuals across the deck look like they belong together?
- Do slides across a deck look like they clearly belong together?
- How's the balance of similarity and variety?

In Sum

- Uncluttered visuals with fewer elements allow viewers to easily see the harmonious relationships among the unifying elements. If the visuals consist of too many objects or too great a variety among objects, your slides will look incongruous.

- Look for the similarities in elements, or how your elements are positioned, to connect your slides. Consider your choices in typeface, font size, and color to help you find a similar, harmonious feel that matches the theme of the content.

- Tie your ideas together by providing meaningful cues to the viewer throughout the presentation. Try using a particular color, recurring shape, particular use of space, poignant line, and so on. These visual (or audio) markers will be useful to your audience and strengthen your message.

- Sometimes the greatest source of creative solutions comes only when we have a structure within which to work. Designing with a grid makes it easier to arrange elements and ultimately offers more freedom to experiment with the elements that comprise our messages. The unity that is created makes for clear, harmonious designs.

the journey

Never discourage anyone...
who continually makes progress,
no matter how slow.

— Plato

10

Slide Samples

In your pursuit to learn more about design in general, and about making better slides in particular, it's important to search out good examples. In my first book, *Presentation Zen,* I included a chapter of slide samples to give readers some inspiration for their own presentations. They proved to be very helpful in demonstrating many of the concepts from the book, so I have included samples here, too. In this chapter, the examples are from a few different presentations (containing partial slide decks, due to space restraints) by presenters and designers who I admire for the powerful ways they make a connection to the audience.

While the slides on the following pages look good design-wise and often contain strong visuals, they also communicate messages in a crystal-clear manner through attention to typography, a good use of space, the intentional use of color, and other things you've been learning about in this book.

By now, you should have a good idea about what makes a slide effective and how to embrace and use ideas such as simplicity, focal point, balance, and unity. Once you have achieved this harmony in your slides, you'll find the design is naturally better and the overall presentation is substantially better.

Takehime Pudding
The Best Sweets in Ikoma, Nara

Akino Ogata

Owner, Pastry Chef
Takehime, Inc.
www.takehime.co.jp

Design: Keiko Noda / Grace-Field
www.grace-field.com

Our good friend Ogata runs a small pastry shop in our neighborhood. Her shop was relatively unknown until she recently won the grand prize for the first official competition to select the best confectionery in our hometown of Ikoma. As our hometown is known for clean water, bamboo, and Japanese sake, she decided to combine all those elements to create a tasteful pudding called "Takehime Pudding." Other more well-known companies entered the competition as well, but presented in the more typical bullet-point driven style. In the end, the judges said the reason she won the grand prize was not only due to the quality of the product but also to how she presented her story and her pitch. It was effective and she stood out. Ogata says she studied ideas from *Presentation Zen,* and then teamed up with a local graphic designer, Keiko Noda, to create visually appealing slides. The approach of the design was to keep things simple and select many high-quality images to tell a story. Ogata's business is continuing to grow thanks in part to her well-prepared, award-winning presentation.

Featured on these two pages are 21 of the original 39 slides used during Ogata's actual live presentation.

銘酒

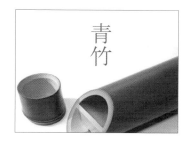
青竹

酒粕

葛

黒豆

酒粕

エコロジー 美肌効果: 血液さらさら

生駒山

4個入り¥1,000

贈答用竹籠 ¥300

新しい 生駒との融合

たけひめプリン

酒粕スティック

酒粕かすてら

酒粕マドレーヌ

The Gulf of Mexico

Matt Stout

NOAA, National Marine Sanctuary

www.sanctuaries.noaa.gov

Design: Duarte, Inc.

The National Oceanic and Atmospheric Administration (NOAA) National Marine Sanctuary group commissioned Duarte Design to create a presentation to motivate policymakers to take action toward securing the Gulf of Mexico as a marine sanctuary. The creative process involved developing three very distinct and broadly varied solutions to communicate the cause. The final solution employed hand-drawn infographics and type overlaid on photos with a distressed texture around the edges that gave the presentation a revolutionary feel. (The slides here represent about a third of the visuals used.)

Smoke: The Convenient Truth
Empowered Presentations

A presentation design firm founded by
Cory Jim and Yancey Unequivocally

empoweredpresentations.com

This slide deck by Empowered Presentations, a presentation design firm in Honolulu, Hawaii, won first prize in Slideshare's World's Best Presentation Contest 2010 in both the Overall Category and in the Education Category. The slides here represent less than half the actual deck. Empowered Presentations used data from sources such as the World Health Organization (WHO) and the Surgeon General, which are cited in the last slide (not shown here).

See the entire deck here at www.slideshare.net/mrcoryjim/smoke-the-convenient-truth-5602255.

Duarte, Inc., shares the process the firm went through to build a file that pushes the limits of PowerPoint features. The best ideas start off as loose sketches.

www.duarte.com

The role of sketching and planning analog

When Microsoft was about to launch PowerPoint 10, the company approached Duarte, Inc., to build a presentation that would come installed with the application. Not only would users be able to deconstruct the file and learn the new features, but they would also see how Duarte combined features to create powerful effects.

The first step Duarte took was to learn all the new features and the limits of the application, then write a script that could showcase those features well. After the script was approved, the artist created an enormous amount of loosely sketched ideas. These loose sketches are what make or break a project. He sketched out several ideas for each sentence in the script. Then he culled the ideas down into scenes and sketched the final scenes into a storyboard.

Anyone can create loose sketches. They are small visual representations of ideas. Because they are loosely drawn, you can create many of them quickly. Take a look below. Even the storyboard lacks detail but it clearly conveys the meaning of what needs to be communicated.

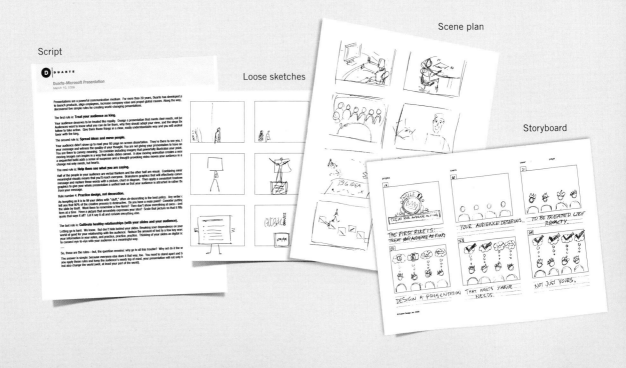

Script

Loose sketches

Scene plan

Storyboard

Duarte created four custom background textures, so when using the Push transition between slides it appeared to be one large textured surface.

Duarte established a retro look. The team also wanted to incorporate a handmade feel, so they made special textures and hand-drawn illustrations and made photos look like they were cut out of paper.

Employees were wrangled into participating in the photo shoot. They mimicked clothing, hairstyles, and accessories of the 1950s. The shoot was done in less than a half-day. By shooting their own images they avoided usage rights concerns.

2 SPREAD **IDEAS** AND MOVE **PEOPLE**

3 HELP THEM **SEE** WHAT YOU ARE **SAYING**

The same employees were shot from behind to create an audience.

Treated photo

Original photo

PowerPoint now has a Film Grain effect. In the sample on the left, the transparency and grain size were adjusted. The Color Tone Temperature was increased using Picture Color Options in the Recolor menu to give the image a warmer color tone.

4 PRACTICE DESIGN NOT DECORATION

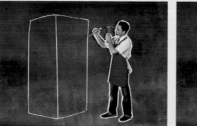

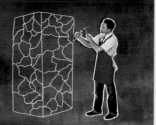

Sketching out a powerful concept can be more useful than going straight to the stock photo sites. This series of images conveys that one of the most important phases in the design process is destructive.

5 CULTIVATE HEALTHY RELATIONSHIPS

Don't hide behind your slides. Practice your presentation until it becomes a seamless backdrop. You may not get to change the entire world, but a great presentation can change your world!

How Bacteria Talk

Dr. Bonnie Bassler

Professor
Department of Molecular Biology
Princeton University

www.molbio1.princeton.edu/labs/bassler/

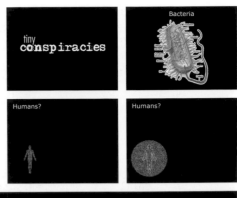

In her 2009 TED talk, Dr. Bassler showed how bacterial "chatter" is not exceptional behavior as was once thought. In fact, most bacteria chatter, and most do it all the time. Dr. Bassler and designer Todd Reichart (who is also her husband) worked together to make the concepts visual for the TED audience.

Dr. Bassler is a wonderful speaker. She says she has a passion for trying to get laypeople to like science—and to not think it's scary or too hard or boring. Her talk was one of the best presentations I attended at TED in Long Beach, California. I was amazed. Dr. Bassler is very good at speaking in a down-to-earth, conversational manner. There is great clarity to her narrative. For example, she often says, "The question is then…" or "So the question is this:…" Along the way she also answers the two questions we often have as listeners: "So what?" and "Why does this matter?" (These are two questions that too often go unanswered.)

I love her style. She never relies on bullet points (there are none), but instead she moves her eyes naturally around the room, clearly engrossed in what she is explaining but also very much in the moment. She references the screen often but only to illustrate her point. She uses her hands a great deal to explain processes, just as you would in ordinary, natural conversation.

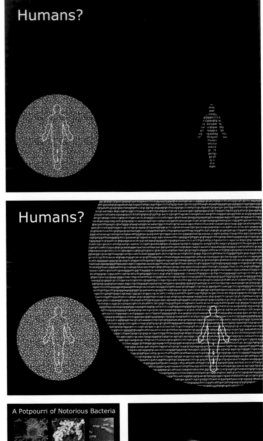

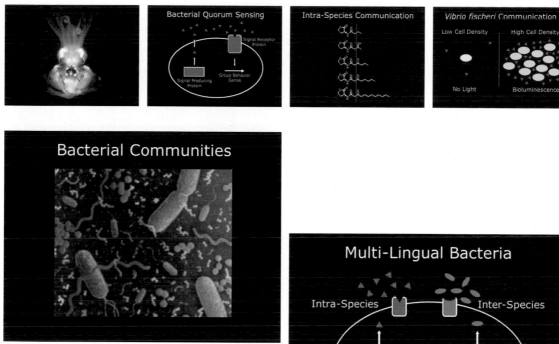

Bacterial Communities

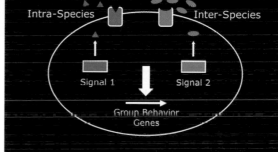

Multi-Lingual Bacteria

Intra-Species   Inter-Species

Signal 1   Signal 2

Group Behavior
Genes

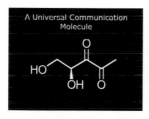

A Universal Communication
Molecule

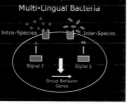

Multi-Lingual Bacteria

Intra-Species   Inter-Species

Signal 1   Signal 2

Group Behavior
Genes

A New Approach to Antibiotics

Virulent Bacteria

Quorum Sensing In Bacteria

Bacteria talk to each other

Bacteria are multi-cellular

Bacteria can distinguish self from other

Develop strategies to impede/improve
quorum sensing

Thirst

Jeff Brenman

Founder and CEO, Apollo Ideas

www.apolloideas.com

This educational presentation by designer Jeff Brenman won first prize in Slideshare's World's Best Presentation Contest 2008. The presentation explores humanity's water use and the emerging worldwide water shortage. It's designed for online viewing. However, in a live talk some of the text could be removed, making the slides a better complement to the speaker's words. Brenman makes good use of high-quality images and big, clean sans serif type. Just a few slides are shown here from a 64-slide presentation. You can find all the slides used in this presentation on Slideshare.net: www.slideshare.net/jbrenman/thirst.

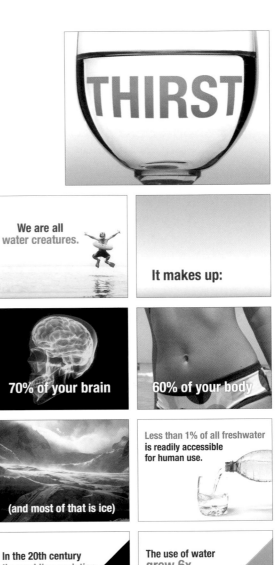

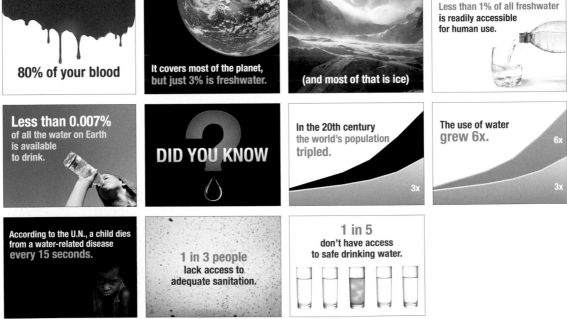

In Sum

Though the content and circumstances are different in each case, what the slides in this chapter have in common is that they are simple, they are highly visual, and they served a successful supportive role in a live talk. The slides augment the presenter's narrative and help make things clear. Here are just a few things to keep in mind as you prepare and design your own slides:

- Develop a clear design priority and make it easy for a viewer to understand the important points in your slides.

- Avoid the death-by-PowerPoint approach and don't clutter your slides with overly complicated graphics, bullet points, and too many color schemes or font choices.

- See and use empty space for a more powerful design that brings clarity to your message.

- Use images and text in interesting ways, but always remember to balance your elements.

- Work animation into your slides for an added layer of emotional impact.

- Look for the similarities as well as the contrasts to bring unity to your slides.

11

Continuous Improvement

The first step in your personal journey of continuous improvement in design is establishing your starting point. The only competition is with yourself. Most of us never learned the design and visual communication strategies we need today. But it's never too late to learn. Regardless of how old you are, you're never too old to learn and improve.

To evaluate your starting point—and later assess your improvement—you need to stop, take time off the grid, and reflect on where you are now and on how you want to improve. In Japan there is a reflection process called *hansei*, which is a kind of downtime of introspection and self-reflection during which people think about the current situation or project—even if things are going well—and brainstorm ways to improve it. Without hansei, there can be no learning. No reflection, no improvement.

Jazz legend Paul Desmond once said, "Writing is like jazz. It can be learned, but it can't be taught." Much the same could be said of design—about learning to see and think more visually. Teachers are necessary and important and they can point the way. But in the end, it's always up to us to learn it, and most of our learning now is a result of our own efforts and our lifelong commitment to continuous improvement through education outside the classroom.

Long-Term Improvement: Kaizen

The Japanese term *kaizen* (改善) means "improvement," literally change + good. In relation to business processes, however, kaizen more closely resembles "continuous improvement." Kaizen is rooted in the principles of total quality management brought to Japan after World War II by statistician W. Edwards Deming and others.

Kaizen is key to the steady improvement and innovation of successful companies in Japan such as Toyota. In the book *The Elegant Solution: Toyota's Formula for Mastering Innovation* (Free Press, 2006), author Matthew May says, "Kaizen is one of those magical concepts that is at once a philosophy, a principle, a practice, and a tool."

Although corporations use kaizen as a tool to achieve greater innovation, productivity, and general excellence, it's also an approach we can learn from and apply to our own lives as we strive for continuous improvement on a more personal level. Let's call this "personal kaizen." You can apply the personal kaizen approach to personal efficiency, also known as GTD—Getting Things Done. You, too, can take the spirit of kaizen and apply it to your unique personal approach to improving—step by step, little by little—your design mindfulness, knowledge, and skill.

Kaizen is daily, continuous, and steady—it takes the long-term view. Kaizen also requires a commitment and a strong willingness to change. I suggest you incorporate it into your approach to learning all you can about design and visual communication over the long term.

The interesting thing about kaizen is that big, sudden improvements are not necessary. Instead, what is important is that you're always looking for ideas— even the smallest ideas—that you can build on. Tiny improvements are OK as over the long term they can add up to great improvements. Each journey begins with a single step, also a precept inherent in kaizen. Simple, doable changes may not seem like much at the time, but they add up.

There is an old saying that goes, "Once you think you have arrived, you have already begun your descent." No matter how good things may seem now, there is always room for improvement. Looking to improve every day is what the spirit of personal kaizen is all about. It's not about how far you have come or how far you have yet to go. It is only about this moment, about being open to seeing the lessons around you, and possessing the capacity and willingness to learn and improve.

The Lessons Are All Around You

The legendary Yogi Berra once said, "You can observe a lot by just watching." Obvious perhaps, yet profound in its simple truth. If you want to improve, learn to see the vast number of lessons all around you. You can learn a lot by really taking the time to see and examine your visual world. Design is everywhere. We can learn tremendous lessons by simply opening our eyes and observing the work of professionals around us. You never know where inspiration or good examples will turn up.

Design is, indeed, everywhere. If you live in an urban environment, you are absolutely surrounded by it and much of it may go unnoticed. Just paying attention to the ubiquitous samples of graphic design—for example, posters, banners, billboards, and signage of all types—could fill every waking moment of your day. This explains why we ignore most of it: because we have other stuff to do. Still, we can learn a great deal by paying attention to our urban (or not-so-urban) environments.

Professional designers tend to be more skilled than most people at noticing "the design" around them. Yet, all of us can improve our design quotient by simply opening our eyes and our minds and peering into the urban backgrounds we may have perceived as visual noise in the past.

To learn from your environment, you have to notice the lessons. But in order to see and take note, you have to be aware. Awareness is the first step to personal kaizen. Most of us lack the ability to remain aware as we hurry through our typical days, filled with myriad forms of what some call multitasking and others call distractions.

Our daily life moves fast, but awareness—the kind of awareness that leads to understanding and growth—needs a slower pace. Learn to set aside time each day, or as often as your busy life permits, to find alone time. Find a time during which you can slow down long enough to see the lessons around you and take special note of them. Over time, you'll begin to strengthen your awareness and the lessons will seem to pop out more and more.

The more you study design principles and the language of design, the more you'll begin to notice examples in your environment—examples you had not seen before even though they were there all along. Slowing down helps increase your awareness, but so does knowledge itself. The increased knowledge you acquire through books, the Web, and other types of informal and formal training, plus the time you set aside to take the slower path, will contribute to profound personal improvement over the long term. Remember: It's a journey.

Observing during the morning commute

We can even learn something during the morning commute. Each day, I generally spend a couple of hours on trains, all of which are filled with an ever-changing tapestry of banners, signs, and ad posters. On most days, I notice something particularly good…or not so good.

No matter where you live, every time you step outside the door you'll find more graphic design to witness. Whether you are on foot, in a car, or using public transportation for your commute to work or school, learn to pay special attention to the posters and other signage you encounter.

Learning from billboards

In the best-selling book *slide:ology: The Art and Science of Creating Great Presentations* (O'Reilly Media, 2008) Nancy Duarte says that good slides are, in many ways, similar to billboards. Like a billboard, the audience should be able to get the meaning quickly. Slides, like billboards, are "glance media."

I am not suggesting that you literally copy the style of a Nike sign or an Apple billboard. You can, however, incorporate the same principles designers use for billboards and other glance media into the visuals that accompany your live talks.

Most people couldn't care less about a billboard or the sign outside a store, but you're different. You're on a journey to learn from your visual environment. So you slow down and you pay attention to "the design of it." You notice the elements, such as color, size, shape, line, pattern, texture, emptiness, alignment, proximity, contrast, and so on, and how the use of these elements contributes to the effectiveness or failure of the design.

Identifying with package design

For many companies, the ROI (return on investment) for package design is much better than for advertising. Packaging is that important. The fundamental functions of packaging include ease of transport (such as bottled tea or a FedEx box), protection, and, of course, identity and communication. In addition, customers have visceral reactions to the visual design of the package itself. Poor package design can overshadow the otherwise good content that may lurk inside. Most successful companies pay close attention to the design of their packaging. You can find lessons hidden in those designs if you take the time to look closely. Here are just two examples from right here in my home in Osaka.

Daniel Kwintner is a designer from Belgium who works for a design firm called IDA here in Osaka. Daniel's design work recently helped his firm win an award for a package design created for a condom manufacturer in Japan. By creating a completely new design that targeted young women rather than men, they helped their client more than double their sales.

The new designs shown here are very different from the old designs, which lacked a concept and were very drab, boring, and "mediciney." The old design was quite symmetrical, typical, and dull. On the new packaging, note the asymmetrical design, the use of white space, and how the implied lines of the butterflies' flight lead the eye to the center brand name—this is where the designer wants the eye to go. The simple, attractive design brings you in, but once you have it in your hand you can then turn it over to get all the details as needed. Simplification is also about moving things away, such as moving detailed information (which becomes clutter) from the front of the package to the back.

Designer Keiko Kobayashi and American entrepreneur Doug Schafer, President of Toyo Beverages in Japan, set out to design a package for their sugar sticks that fit the company's brand. The new box shown here makes good use of empty space and shows the product in a way that leads the eyes to the center logo and name. Says Schafer: "We were trying to achieve something visually eye-catching while allowing the customer to know what was inside the package. The package also allowed for versatility as you could turn it three ways so each retailer could display it in a slightly different way if needed to meet their needs and ours."

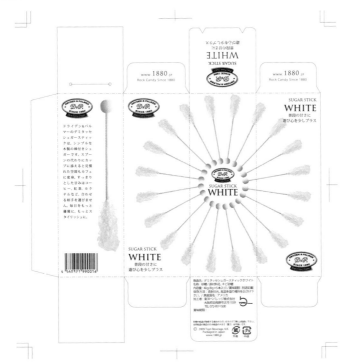

Noticing brochures and other printed material

Magazines, catalogs, brochures, and other printed material are everywhere, but do we ever notice their design? The designer of a concert poster or a company's annual report has a similar goal: to attract the audience's attention and to keep their attention while helping them understand the material in the most effective and memorable way possible. You can learn a lot by using your critical eye to evaluate the impact and effectiveness of the printed material you encounter.

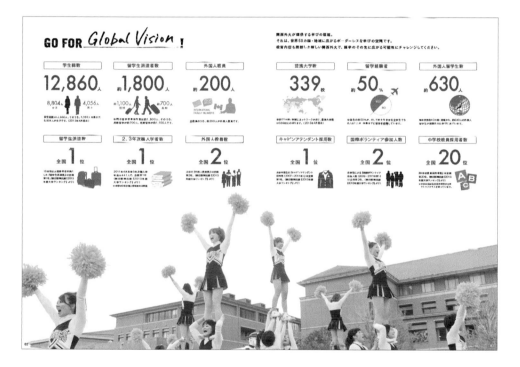

This is the opening spread of a very nice, 32-page recruitment piece for Kansai Gaidai University in Japan. You'll notice the high-impact photograph first, but the implied line formed by the cheerleaders leads the eye to the infographic elements at the top of the page. The content at the top highlights—at a glance—the key selling points of the university.

The large photograph gets your attention and puts a face on the content of the text, which refers to the student's acceptance into flight school for a major airline. Notice the eye gaze and the direction of the hand-drawn airplane. The eye gaze also takes the reader to the next page.

This page uses a dynamic mix of photography and vector graphics at the top to give the basic information in a more visual and memorable way than merely listing it in bullet-point form.

As you turn to this two-page spread in the same brochure your eyes may glance to the right first but will quickly go to the large image of the student. The student's eye gaze takes you smoothly to the copy on the left. Then, if you are interested in more detail about this particular program, you can spend time exploring detail information on the right page.

This example comes from Akihiro Tsuchiya, a senior at Kansai Gaidai University and one of my former students who took a keen interest in one of my design classes. Tsuchiya was responsible for creating a poster to place around campus that encouraged visiting high school students to drop by one of the buildings from 12:30–3 p.m. to talk with current Japanese and foreign students. His first attempt (left), made in PowerPoint, was printed on A3-size paper—rather small for getting attention. By including three photos, each with several smaller elements, the poster fails to be noticed and understood as glance media. His second attempt (below) is much better. Using PowerPoint again, he created four different designs with the same look and feel of other forms of university communications. The new posters were 50 x 35 inches and printed on an industrial printer. The photographs are now large enough to be noticed and understood in an instant.

AFTER ▼

Finding inspiration out on the street

I usually have my iPhone with me, so any time something catches my eye, I can take a quick snap of it. Sometimes I go for walks in the city with a better camera with the sole purpose of finding good and bad examples of graphic design from which to learn. Often, I snap a photo and immediately send it to one of my blogs (garr.posterous.com) to share with my readers. Later, I may use the pictures in presentations or training seminars. Take a look at a few snapshots from my home city of Osaka, Japan, that I use for inspiration.

Jogging near Osaka Castle, I take note of the juxtaposition: the old castle tower on the left and the new high-rise buildings on the right, separated (or united?) by a moat.

This map uses black and white, shades of gray, and key highlight colors with only enough detail to be useful.

What could be simpler than Helvetica black on a white sign? In a sea of signage, it actually stands out.

Word Art: It's (still) everywhere. It reminds us that we must refrain from decorating a sign or a slide.

Here are examples of signage with a clear hierarchy that leads the eyes. Notice how the Japanese and English type works in harmony by keeping the English text close to the Japanese it belongs with but at a clearly smaller (but legible) size. A similar technique can be used in slides.

Most menus in Japan show photos of all or most of the items. And why not? We are visual beings. Whenever possible, make it visual for greater clarity.

Free coffee! Get it?

I captured a good example of contrast in the office at work. The new employee is bright red and of an unusual shape.

Tips for Long-Term, Continuous Improvement

Personal kaizen is a long-term pursuit of education and growth. Key concepts include awareness, mindfulness, and a willingness to change and make small improvements virtually every day to your own knowledge base and abilities. You can do many small things to increase your design mindfulness and skills over time. The following are just a few:

• Keep an analog scrapbook of examples of good and bad designs. This includes anything from napkins and paper cups to business cards and brochures, flyers, and posters—whatever you find remarkable that fits inside a folder, box, or scrapbook. From time to time, review your analog examples and reflect on what works, what doesn't, and why. This activity is even better in a group where people come together and share their scrapbook contents in a design show-and-tell session.

• Keep a digital scrapbook in the form of an online photo blog—either private or open to anyone—where you store interesting examples of design. Usually, you can take a snapshot and then upload it to your blog right from your phone. (Of course, be careful of people's right to privacy when taking snapshots outside.)

• Record your observations digitally. When an idea snaps into your head or you notice something that stimulates your imagination, use a voice recorder to record the idea (your phone may have one). It may seem odd, but I often even go jogging with my iPhone just in case I need to take a picture of something remarkable or an idea comes to mind that I need to record instantly.

• Keep stimulating the right side of your brain by learning a musical instrument or rediscovering an instrument you used to play. Playing music is one of those creative "whole brain" activities that enriches your life (and your work). You are never too old to learn to play an instrument.

• Get completely unplugged and off the grid—
no iPhones and the like. Go for a walk, a hike,
a bike ride, or whatever it is that allows you to
slow your busy mind. What if a brilliant idea hits
you and you can't record it? What if you see a
remarkable example and can't take a picture of
it? Don't worry about it. Getting off the grid and
freeing up your mind (and pockets) is necessary
for the flow of ideas, too.

• When you go for walks in nature, keep a keen eye
out for the balance, colors, lines, shapes, and so
forth that most people never notice. What visual
lessons exist in stopping to look at the whole and
then zooming in to look at the particular? There is
much to be learned by careful observation of nature.

Your journey includes time off the grid, too.

• Take an art class at a local community college
or university. Don't worry that it may not have
"obvious applications for work." The art—whatever
it is—will teach you lessons about seeing and
communicating through form. All you need to do is
practice and enjoy the journey. You'll find, perhaps
unexpectedly, that there are indeed lessons you
can apply to your own work or personal life.

• Take some time to examine packages in stores,
regardless of whether you are interested in the
product. What catches your eye as you walk
through a shop? Nothing is by accident, so
think about what the designers were trying to
communicate with the package.

- Teach others what you learn. One of the best ways to deepen and solidify your new knowledge is to teach it to others. Give a presentation in your town such as at a Pecha Kucha night, Ignite night, TEDx Conference, or your local Toastmasters meeting. Run a seminar, teach a class, or volunteer to run a small internal workshop to teach others in your organization what you are learning. Real learning occurs when you share it. Share your new knowledge and passion about design in a short presentation.

- Make it a point to watch TED videos online (www.ted.com), especially those related to design and creativity. Many of the presenters use very effective, well-designed visuals. Subscribe to the TED RSS feed or follow TED on Twitter.

- Read books on graphic design, typography, color, photography, documentary filmmaking, and even architecture and other areas of design—you never know where the design lessons are to be found. I link to many of my favorite books on the Presentation Zen Web site (www.presentationzen.com).

It's All Up to You Now

Good ideas and information are necessary conditions for an effective presentation. Design also matters. But design is not about dazzle, sizzle, or slickness. Design is about clarity, evidence, engagement, and story. If the content has structure—if it's true and honest and designed with the audience or end user in mind—then chances are it will be an attractive design as well. It's not an issue of substance over style. The issue is how we design visuals and other messages that are in balance and in harmony with our narrative in a way that amplifies and augments our spoken words. There is no one right way to do it. The best style is the result of careful reflection on the material and the audience, and the selection of a creative approach that is the simplest without being simplistic. A design that is too simple can be just as confusing as information overload. The key word is always balance. In all things: balance.

We're in a time in which it's more crucial than ever to use credible information, research, and evidence in our talks, and to present our content visually in a way that is engaging, clear, and memorable. If your ideas are worth spreading, then presentation matters. And if you are using visuals to amplify your presentation, then design matters.

頑張ってください！

good luck!

Photo Credits

iStockphoto and Pixta

The iStockphoto and Pixta images that appear on these pages were used to enhance the presentation of the book. You can find the exact photo at iStockphoto.com or Pixtastock.com by conducting a search using the unique number code for the image.

Cover photo   **Chapter 1**

Chapter 2

istockphoto.com
5518167

istockphoto.com
2743609

istockphoto.com
20061416

istockphoto.com
10539585

pixtastock.com
2161131

istockphoto.com
21081280

istockphoto.com
18197539

istockphoto.com
19055591

Chapter 3

Chapter 4   **Chapter 5**   **Chapter 6**

pixtastock.com
1014189

istockphoto.com
745511

istockphoto.com
9957519

istockphoto.com
22678256

istockphoto.com
24347403

istockphoto.com
27601209

istockphoto.com
467365

istockphoto.com
10215093

Chapter 7

Chapter 8   **Chapter 9**

pixtastock.com
2242915

istockphoto.com
2687317

istockphoto.com
7108572

istockphoto.com
6645843

istockphoto.com
16997244

istockphoto.com
9713681

istockphoto.com
3081682

istockphoto.com
2783526

Chapter 10   **Chapter 11**

pixtastock.com
8217563

pixtastock.com
973962

istockphoto.com
10053110

istockphoto.com
4451265

istockphoto.com
18935390

Hiyoshiya Co., Ltd.

Wagasa images on the last page of each chapter courtesy of Mr. Kotaro Nishibori, Hiyoshiya Co., Ltd. in Kyoto, Japan.
www.wagasa.com

Index

Numbers

BREAKING: CLIENT KNOWS IT WHEN HE SEES IT.

It's easier to find "it" with millions of
original files available only from iStock.

Visit iStock.com/presentationzendesign and save 20% on credits.